Spring: Microservices with Spring Boot

Unlock the power of Spring Boot to build and deploy production-ready microservices

Ranga Rao Karanam

BIRMINGHAM - MUMBAI

Spring: Microservices with Spring Boot

First published: March 2018

Production reference: 1090318

Published by Packt Publishing Ltd.
Livery Place, 35 Livery Street
Birmingham B3 2PB, UK.

ISBN: 978-1-78913-258-8

www.packtpub.com

Credits

This book is a blend of text and quizzes, all packaged up keeping your journey in mind. It includes content from the following Packt product:

- *Mastering Spring 5.0* by *Ranga Rao Karanam*

Meet Your Expert

We have the best work of the following esteemed author to ensure that your learning journey is smooth:

Ranga Rao Karanam is a programmer, trainer, and architect. His areas of interest include cloud native applications, microservices, evolutionary design, high-quality code, DevOps, BDD, TDD, and refactoring. He loves consulting for startups on developing scalable, component-based cloud native applications, and following modern development practices such as BDD, continuous delivery, and DevOps. He loves the freedom the Spring Framework brings to developing enterprise Java applications. Ranga started in28minutes with the vision of creating high-quality courses on developing cloud native Java applications. He is looking forward to enhancing his already considerable success--75,000 students on Udemy and 35,000 subscribers on YouTube.

Table of Contents

Preface

Nowadays developers are facing competitive pressures and it impacts the way they build applications, which includes faster delivery, scalability, and high performance. Microservices helps in decomposing applications into small services and move away from a single monolithic artifact. In that case, we can build systems that are scalable, flexible, and high resilient. Spring Boot helps in building such REST-oriented, production-grade microservices.

So, if you want to build microservices with Spring Boot, you are in the right path.

What's in It for Me?

Maps are vital for your journey, especially when you're holidaying in another continent. When it comes to learning, a roadmap helps you in giving a definitive path for progressing towards the goal. So, here you're presented with a roadmap before you begin your journey.

This book is meticulously designed and developed in order to empower you with all the right and relevant information on Spring Boot. We've created this Learning Path for you that consists of three lessons:

Lesson 1, Building Microservices with Spring Boot, covers the basics of Spring Boot and REST services. You will explore different features of Spring Boot and create a few REST services with great tests.

Lesson 2, Extending Microservices, covers how to add features such as exception handling, caching, and internationalization to your application. You will learn the best practices of documenting REST services using Swagger. You will look at the basics of securing your microservices with Spring Security.

Lesson 3, Advanced Spring Boot Features, takes a look at the advanced features in Spring Boot. You will learn how to monitor a microservice with a Spring Boot Actuator. You will then learn how to deploy the microservice to Cloud. You will also learn how to develop more effectively with the developer tools provided by Spring Boot.

What Will I Get from This Book?

- Use Spring Initializr to create a basic Spring project
- Build a basic microservice with Spring Boot
- Implement caching and exception handling
- Secure your microservice with Spring security and OAuth2
- Deploy microservices using self-contained HTTP server
- Monitor your microservices with Spring Boot actuator
- Learn to develop more effectively with developer tools

Prerequisites

This book is aimed at Java developers who knows the basics of Spring programming and want to build microservices with Spring Boot. Some of the prerequisites that is required before you begin this book are:

- Working knowledge on Java
- Basic knowledge on Spring programming

1
Building Microservices with Spring Boot

As we discussed in the last lesson, we are moving toward architectures with smaller, independently deployable microservices. This would mean that there will be a huge number of smaller microservices developed.

An important consequence is that we would need to be able to quickly get off the ground and get running with new components.

Spring Boot aims to solve the problem of getting off fast with a new component. In this lesson, we will start with understanding the capabilities Spring Boot brings to the table. We will answer the following questions:

- Why Spring Boot?
- What are the features that Spring Boot provides?
- What is auto-configuration?
- What is Spring Boot not?
- What happens in the background when you use Spring Boot?
- How do you use Spring Initializr to create new Spring Boot projects?
- How do you create basic RESTful services with Spring Boot?

What is Spring Boot?

First of all, let's start with clearing out a few misconceptions about Spring Boot:

- Spring Boot is not a code generation framework. It does not generate any code.
- Spring Boot is neither an application server, nor is it a web server. It provides good integration with different ranges of applications and web servers.
- Spring Boot does not implement any specific frameworks or specifications.

These questions still remain:

- What is Spring Boot?
- Why has it become so popular in the last couple of years?

To answer these questions, let's build a quick example. Let's consider an example application that you want to quickly prototype.

Building a Quick Prototype for a Microservice

Let's say we want to build a microservice with Spring MVC and use JPA (with Hibernate as the implementation) to connect to the database.

Let's consider the steps in setting up such an application:

1. Decide which versions of Spring MVC, JPA and Hibernate to use.
2. Set up a Spring context to wire all the different layers together.
3. Set up a web layer with Spring MVC (including Spring MVC configuration):
    - Configure beans for DispatcherServlet, handler, resolvers, view resolvers, and so on
4. Set up Hibernate in the data layer:
    - Configure beans for SessionFactory, data source, and so on
5. Decide and implement how to store your application configuration, which varies between different environments.
6. Decide how you would want to do your unit testing.
7. Decide and implement your transaction management strategy.
8. Decide and implement how to implement security.
9. Set up your logging framework.

10. Decide and implement how you want to monitor your application in production.

11. Decide and implement a metrics management system to provide statistics about the application.

12. Decide and implement how to deploy your application to a web or application server.

At least a few of the steps mentioned have to be completed before we can start with building our business logic. And this might take a few weeks at the least.

When we build microservices, we would want to make a quick start. All the preceding steps will not make it easy to develop a microservice. And that's the problem Spring Boot aims to solve.

The following quote is an extract from the Spring Boot website (`http://docs.spring.io/spring-boot/docs/current-SNAPSHOT/reference/htmlsingle/#boot-documentation`):

> *Spring Boot makes it easy to create stand-alone, production-grade Spring based applications that you can "just run". We take an opinionated view of the Spring platform and third-party libraries so you can get started with minimum fuss. Most Spring Boot applications need very little Spring configuration*
>
> *Spring Boot enables developers to focus on the business logic behind their microservice. It aims to take care of all the nitty-gritty technical details involved in developing microservices.*

Primary Goals

The primary goals of Spring Boot are as follows:

- Enable quickly getting off the ground with Spring-based projects.
- Be opinionated. Make default assumptions based on common usage. Provide configuration options to handle deviations from defaults.
- Provide a wide range of nonfunctional features out of the box.
- Do not use code generation and avoid using a lot of XML configuration.

Nonfunctional Features

A few of the nonfunctional features provided by Spring Boot are as follows:

- Default handling of versioning and configuration of a wide range of frameworks, servers, and specifications
- Default options for application security
- Default application metrics with possibilities to extend
- Basic application monitoring using health checks
- Multiple options for externalized configuration

Spring Boot Hello World

We will start with building our first Spring Boot application in this lesson. We will use Maven to manage dependencies.

The following steps are involved in starting up with a Spring Boot application:

1. Configure `spring-boot-starter-parent` in your `pom.xml` file.
2. Configure the `pom.xml` file with the required starter projects.
3. Configure `spring-boot-maven-plugin` to be able to run the application.
4. Create your first Spring Boot launch class.

Let's start with step 1, configuring the starter projects.

Configure spring-boot-starter-parent

Let's start with a simple `pom.xml` file with `spring-boot-starter-parent`:

```xml
<project xmlns="http://maven.apache.org/POM/4.0.0"
 xmlns:xsi="http://www.w3.org/2001/XMLSchema-instance"
 xsi:schemaLocation="http://maven.apache.org/POM/4.0.0
 http://maven.apache.org/xsd/maven-4.0.0.xsd">
<modelVersion>4.0.0</modelVersion>
<groupId>com.mastering.spring</groupId>
<artifactId>springboot-example</artifactId>
<version>0.0.1-SNAPSHOT</version>
<name>First Spring Boot Example</name>
<packaging>war</packaging>
<parent>
   <groupId>org.springframework.boot</groupId>
   <artifactId>spring-boot-starter-parent</artifactId>
```

```xml
        <version>2.0.0.M1</version>
    </parent>
    <properties>
        <java.version>1.8</java.version>
    </properties>

  <repositories>
   <repository>
      <id>spring-milestones</id>
      <name>Spring Milestones</name>
      <url>https://repo.spring.io/milestone</url>
      <snapshots>
        <enabled>false</enabled>
      </snapshots>
   </repository>
  </repositories>

  <pluginRepositories>
   <pluginRepository>
      <id>spring-milestones</id>
      <name>Spring Milestones</name>
      <url>https://repo.spring.io/milestone</url>
        <snapshots>
          <enabled>false</enabled>
        </snapshots>
    </pluginRepository>
   </pluginRepositories>

   </project>
```

The first question is this: why do we need `spring-boot-starter-parent`?

A `spring-boot-starter-parent` dependency contains the default versions of Java to use, the default versions of dependencies that Spring Boot uses, and the default configuration of the Maven plugins.

 The `spring-boot-starter-parent` dependency is the parent POM providing dependency and plugin management for Spring Boot-based applications.

Let's look at some of the code inside `spring-boot-starter-parent` to get a deeper understanding about `spring-boot-starter-parent`.

spring-boot-starter-parent

The `spring-boot-starter-parent` dependency inherits from `spring-boot-dependencies`, which is defined at the top of the POM. The following code snippet shows an extract from `spring-boot-starter-parent`:

```
<parent>
    <groupId>org.springframework.boot</groupId>
    <artifactId>spring-boot-dependencies</artifactId>
    <version>2.0.0.M1</version>
    <relativePath>../../spring-boot-dependencies</relativePath>
</parent>
```

The `spring-boot-dependencies` provides default dependency management for all the dependencies that Spring Boot uses. The following code shows the different versions of various dependencies that are configured in `spring-boot-dependencies`:

```
<activemq.version>5.13.4</activemq.version>
<aspectj.version>1.8.9</aspectj.version>
<ehcache.version>2.10.2.2.21</ehcache.version>
<elasticsearch.version>2.3.4</elasticsearch.version>
<gson.version>2.7</gson.version>
<h2.version>1.4.192</h2.version>
<hazelcast.version>3.6.4</hazelcast.version>
<hibernate.version>5.0.9.Final</hibernate.version>
<hibernate-validator.version>5.2.4.Final</hibernate
  validator.version>
<hsqldb.version>2.3.3</hsqldb.version>
<htmlunit.version>2.21</htmlunit.version>
<jackson.version>2.8.1</jackson.version>
<jersey.version>2.23.1</jersey.version>
<jetty.version>9.3.11.v20160721</jetty.version>
<junit.version>4.12</junit.version>
<mockito.version>1.10.19</mockito.version>
<selenium.version>2.53.1</selenium.version>
<servlet-api.version>3.1.0</servlet-api.version>
<spring.version>4.3.2.RELEASE</spring.version>
<spring-amqp.version>1.6.1.RELEASE</spring-amqp.version>
<spring-batch.version>3.0.7.RELEASE</spring-batch.version>
<spring-data-releasetrain.version>Hopper-SR2</spring-
  data-releasetrain.version>
<spring-hateoas.version>0.20.0.RELEASE</spring-hateoas.version>
<spring-restdocs.version>1.1.1.RELEASE</spring-restdocs.version>
<spring-security.version>4.1.1.RELEASE</spring-security.version>
```

```
<spring-session.version>1.2.1.RELEASE</spring-session.version>
<spring-ws.version>2.3.0.RELEASE</spring-ws.version>
<thymeleaf.version>2.1.5.RELEASE</thymeleaf.version>
<tomcat.version>8.5.4</tomcat.version>
<xml-apis.version>1.4.01</xml-apis.version>
```

If we want to override a specific version of a dependency, we can do that by providing a property with the right name in the `pom.xml` file of our application. The following code snippet shows an example of configuring our application to use version 1.10.20 of Mockito:

```
<properties>
 <mockito.version>1.10.20</mockito.version>
</properties>
```

The following are some of the other things defined in `spring-boot-starter-parent`:

- The default Java version `<java.version>1.8</java.version>`
- The default configuration for Maven plugins:
    - `maven-failsafe-plugin`
    - `maven-surefire-plugin`
    - `git-commit-id-plugin`

Compatibility between different versions of frameworks is one of the major problems faced by developers. How do I find the latest Spring Session version that is compatible with a specific version of Spring? The usual answer would be to read the documentation. However, if we use Spring Boot, this is made simple by `spring-boot-starter-parent`. If we want to upgrade to a newer Spring version, all that we need to do is to find the `spring-boot-starter-parent` dependency for that Spring version. Once we upgrade our application to use that specific version of `spring-boot-starter-parent`, we would have all the other dependencies upgraded to the versions compatible with the new Spring version. One less problem for developers to handle. Always make me happy.

Configure pom.xml with the Required Starter Projects

Whenever we want to build an application in Spring Boot, we would need to start looking for starter projects. Let's focus on understanding what a starter project is.

Understanding Starter Projects

Starters are simplified dependency descriptors customized for different purposes. For example, `spring-boot-starter-web` is the starter for building web application, including RESTful, using Spring MVC. It uses Tomcat as the default embedded container. If I want to develop a web application using Spring MVC, all we would need to do is include `spring-boot-starter-web` in our dependencies, and we get the following automatically pre-configured:

* Spring MVC

* Compatible versions of `jackson-databind` (for binding) and hibernate-validator (for form validation)

* `spring-boot-starter-tomcat` (starter project for Tomcat)

The following code snippet shows some of the dependencies configured in `spring-boot-starter-web`:

```xml
<dependencies>
    <dependency>
        <groupId>org.springframework.boot</groupId>
        <artifactId>spring-boot-starter</artifactId>
    </dependency>
    <dependency>
        <groupId>org.springframework.boot</groupId>
        <artifactId>spring-boot-starter-tomcat</artifactId>
    </dependency>
    <dependency>
        <groupId>org.hibernate</groupId>
        <artifactId>hibernate-validator</artifactId>
    </dependency>
    <dependency>
        <groupId>com.fasterxml.jackson.core</groupId>
        <artifactId>jackson-databind</artifactId>
    </dependency>
    <dependency>
        <groupId>org.springframework</groupId>
        <artifactId>spring-web</artifactId>
    </dependency>
    <dependency>
        <groupId>org.springframework</groupId>
        <artifactId>spring-webmvc</artifactId>
    </dependency>
</dependencies>
```

As we can see in the preceding snippet, when we use spring-boot-starter-web, we get a lot of frameworks auto-configured.

For the web application we would like to build, we would also want to do some good unit testing and deploy it on Tomcat. The following snippet shows the different starter dependencies that we would need. We would need to add this to our pom.xml file:

```
<dependencies>
  <dependency>
    <groupId>org.springframework.boot</groupId>
    <artifactId>spring-boot-starter-web</artifactId>
  </dependency>
  <dependency>
    <groupId>org.springframework.boot</groupId>
    <artifactId>spring-boot-starter-test</artifactId>
    <scope>test</scope>
  </dependency>
  <dependency>
    <groupId>org.springframework.boot</groupId>
    <artifactId>spring-boot-starter-tomcat</artifactId>
    <scope>provided</scope>
  </dependency>
</dependencies>
```

We add three starter projects:

- We've already discussed spring-boot-starter-web. It provides us with the frameworks needed to build a web application with Spring MVC.

- The spring-boot-starter-test dependency provides the following test frameworks needed for unit testing:
    - **JUnit**: Basic unit test framework
    - **Mockito**: For mocking
    - **Hamcrest, AssertJ**: For readable asserts
    - **Spring Test**: A unit testing framework for spring-context based applications

- The spring-boot-starter-tomcat dependency is the default for running web applications. We include it for clarity. The spring-boot-starter-tomcat is the starter for using Tomcat as the embedded servlet container.

We now have our `pom.xml` file configured with the starter parent and the required starter projects. Let's add `spring-boot-maven-plugin` now, which would enable us to run Spring Boot applications.

Configuring spring-boot-maven-plugin

When we build applications using Spring Boot, there are a couple of situations that are possible:

- We would want to run the applications in place without building a JAR or a WAR
- We would want to build a JAR and a WAR for later deployment

The `spring-boot-maven-plugin` dependency provides capabilities for both of the preceding situations. The following snippet shows how we can configure `spring-boot-maven-plugin` in an application:

```
<build>
 <plugins>
  <plugin>
    <groupId>org.springframework.boot</groupId>
    <artifactId>spring-boot-maven-plugin</artifactId>
  </plugin>
 </plugins>
</build>
```

The `spring-boot-maven-plugin` dependency provides several goals for a Spring Boot application. The most popular goal is run (this can be executed as `mvn spring-boot:run` on the command prompt from the root folder of the project).

Creating Your First Spring Boot Launch Class

The following class explains how to create a simple Spring Boot launch class. It uses the static run method from the `SpringApplication` class, as shown in the following code snippet:

```
package com.mastering.spring.springboot;
import org.springframework.boot.SpringApplication;
import org.springframework.boot
autoconfigure.SpringBootApplication;
import org.springframework.context.ApplicationContext;
@SpringBootApplication public class Application {
   public static void main(String[] args)
    {
```

```
        ApplicationContext ctx = SpringApplication.run
        (Application.class,args);
    }
}
```

The preceding code is a simple Java `main` method executing the static `run` method on the `SpringApplication` class.

The SpringApplication Class

The `SpringApplication` class can be used to Bootstrap and launch a Spring application from a Java `main` method.

The following are the steps that are typically performed when a Spring Boot application is bootstrapped:

1. Create an instance of Spring's `ApplicationContext`.
2. Enable the functionality to accept command-line arguments and expose them as Spring properties.
3. Load all the Spring beans as per the configuration.

The @SpringBootApplication Annotation

The `@SpringBootApplication` annotation is a shortcut for three annotations:

- `@Configuration`: Indicates that this a Spring application context configuration file.

- `@EnableAutoConfiguration`: Enables auto-configuration, an important feature of Spring Boot. We will discuss auto-configuration later in a separate section.

- `@ComponentScan`: Enables scanning for Spring beans in the package of this class and all its sub packages.

Running Our Hello World Application

We can run the Hello World application in multiple ways. Let's start running it with the simplest option--running as a Java application. In your IDE, right-click on the application **class** and run it as **Java Application**. The following screenshot shows some of the log from running our `Hello World` application:

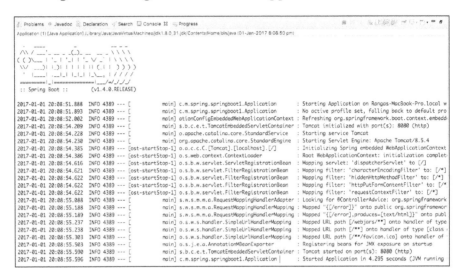

The following are the key things to note:

- Tomcat server is launched on port `8080`--`Tomcat started on port(s): 8080 (http)`.

- `DispatcherServlet` is configured. This means that Spring MVC Framework is ready to accept requests--`Mapping servlet: 'dispatcherServlet' to [/]`.

- Four filters--`characterEncodingFilter`, `hiddenHttpMethodFilter`, `httpPutFormContentFilter` and `requestContextFilter`--are enabled by default

- The default error page is configured--`Mapped "{[/error]}" onto public org.springframework.http.ResponseEntity<java.util.Map<java.lang.String, java.lang.Object>> org.springframework.boot.autoconfigure.web.BasicErrorController.error(javax.servlet.http.HttpServletRequest)`

- WebJars are autoconfigured. WebJars enable dependency management for static dependencies such as Bootstrap and query--`Mapped URL path [/webjars/**] onto handler of type [class org.springframework.web.servlet.resource.ResourceHttpRequestHandler]`

The following screenshot shows the application layout as of now. We have just two files, pom.xml and Application.java:

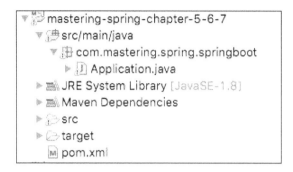

With a simple pom.xml file and one Java class, we were able to get to launch the Spring MVC application, with all the preceding functionality described. The most important thing about Spring Boot is to understand what happens in the background. Understanding the preceding start up log is the first. Let's look at the Maven dependencies to get a deeper picture.

The following screenshot shows some of the dependencies that are configured with the basic configuration in the pom.xml file that we created:

Spring Boot does a lot of magic. Once you have the application configured and running, I recommend that you play around with it to gain a deeper understanding that will be useful when you are debugging problems.

As Spiderman says, with great power, comes great responsibility. This is absolutely true in the case of Spring Boot. In the time to come, the best developers with Spring Boot would be the ones who understand what happens in the background-- dependencies and auto-configuration.

Auto-configuration

To enable us to understand auto-configuration further, let's expand our application class to include a few more lines of code:

```
ApplicationContext ctx = SpringApplication.run(Application.class,
 args);
String[] beanNames = ctx.getBeanDefinitionNames();
Arrays.sort(beanNames);

for (String beanName : beanNames) {
  System.out.println(beanName);
}
```

We get all the beans that are defined in the Spring application context and print their names. When `Application.java` is run as a Java program, it prints the list of beans, as shown in the following output:

```
application
basicErrorController
beanNameHandlerMapping
beanNameViewResolver
characterEncodingFilter
conventionErrorViewResolver
defaultServletHandlerMapping
defaultViewResolver
dispatcherServlet
dispatcherServletRegistration
duplicateServerPropertiesDetector
embeddedServletContainerCustomizerBeanPostProcessor
error
errorAttributes
errorPageCustomizer
errorPageRegistrarBeanPostProcessor
faviconHandlerMapping
faviconRequestHandler
handlerExceptionResolver
hiddenHttpMethodFilter
httpPutFormContentFilter
httpRequestHandlerAdapter
```

```
jacksonObjectMapper
jacksonObjectMapperBuilder
jsonComponentModule
localeCharsetMappingsCustomizer
mappingJackson2HttpMessageConverter
mbeanExporter
mbeanServer
messageConverters
multipartConfigElement
multipartResolver
mvcContentNegotiationManager
mvcConversionService
mvcPathMatcher
mvcResourceUrlProvider
mvcUriComponentsContributor
mvcUrlPathHelper
mvcValidator
mvcViewResolver
objectNamingStrategy
autoconfigure.AutoConfigurationPackages
autoconfigure.PropertyPlaceholderAutoConfiguration
autoconfigure.condition.BeanTypeRegistry
autoconfigure.context.ConfigurationPropertiesAutoConfiguration
autoconfigure.info.ProjectInfoAutoConfiguration
autoconfigure.internalCachingMetadataReaderFactory
autoconfigure.jackson.JacksonAutoConfiguration
autoconfigure.jackson.JacksonAutoConfiguration$Jackson2ObjectMapper
BuilderCustomizerConfiguration
autoconfigure.jackson.JacksonAutoConfiguration$JacksonObjectMapper
BuilderConfiguration
autoconfigure.jackson.JacksonAutoConfiguration$JacksonObject
MapperConfiguration
autoconfigure.jmx.JmxAutoConfiguration
autoconfigure.web.DispatcherServletAutoConfiguration
autoconfigure.web.DispatcherServletAutoConfiguration$Dispatcher
ServletConfiguration
autoconfigure.web.DispatcherServletAutoConfiguration$
DispatcherServletRegistrationConfiguration
autoconfigure.web.EmbeddedServletContainerAutoConfiguration
autoconfigure.web.EmbeddedServletContainerAutoConfiguration$
EmbeddedTomcat
autoconfigure.web.ErrorMvcAutoConfiguration
autoconfigure.web.ErrorMvcAutoConfiguration$WhitelabelError
ViewConfiguration
autoconfigure.web.HttpEncodingAutoConfiguration
```

```
autoconfigure.web.HttpMessageConvertersAutoConfiguration
autoconfigure.web.HttpMessageConvertersAutoConfiguration$String
HttpMessageConverterConfiguration
autoconfigure.web.JacksonHttpMessageConvertersConfiguration
autoconfigure.web.JacksonHttpMessageConvertersConfiguration$MappingJa
ckson2Http
MessageConverterConfiguration
autoconfigure.web.MultipartAutoConfiguration
autoconfigure.web.ServerPropertiesAutoConfiguration
autoconfigure.web.WebClientAutoConfiguration
autoconfigure.web.WebClientAutoConfiguration$RestTemplate
Configuration
autoconfigure.web.WebMvcAutoConfiguration
autoconfigure.web.WebMvcAutoConfiguration$Enable
WebMvcConfiguration
autoconfigure.web.WebMvcAutoConfiguration$WebMvcAuto
ConfigurationAdapter
autoconfigure.web.WebMvcAutoConfiguration$WebMvcAuto
ConfigurationAdapter$FaviconConfiguration
autoconfigure.websocket.WebSocketAutoConfiguration
autoconfigure.websocket.WebSocketAutoConfiguration$
TomcatWebSocketConfiguration
context.properties.ConfigurationPropertiesBindingPostProcessor
context.properties.ConfigurationPropertiesBindingPostProcessor.store
annotation.ConfigurationClassPostProcessor.enhanced
ConfigurationProcessor
annotation.ConfigurationClassPostProcessor.importAwareProcessor
annotation.internalAutowiredAnnotationProcessor
annotation.internalCommonAnnotationProcessor
annotation.internalConfigurationAnnotationProcessor
annotation.internalRequiredAnnotationProcessor
event.internalEventListenerFactory
event.internalEventListenerProcessor
preserveErrorControllerTargetClassPostProcessor
propertySourcesPlaceholderConfigurer
requestContextFilter
requestMappingHandlerAdapter
requestMappingHandlerMapping
resourceHandlerMapping
restTemplateBuilder
serverProperties
simpleControllerHandlerAdapter
spring.http.encoding-autoconfigure.web.HttpEncodingProperties
spring.http.multipart-autoconfigure.web.MultipartProperties
spring.info-autoconfigure.info.ProjectInfoProperties
```

```
spring.jackson-autoconfigure.jackson.JacksonProperties
spring.mvc-autoconfigure.web.WebMvcProperties
spring.resources-autoconfigure.web.ResourceProperties
standardJacksonObjectMapperBuilderCustomizer
stringHttpMessageConverter
tomcatEmbeddedServletContainerFactory
viewControllerHandlerMapping
viewResolver
websocketContainerCustomizer
```

Important things to think about are as follows:

- Where are these beans defined?
- How are these beans created?

That's the magic of Spring auto-configuration.

Whenever we add a new dependency to a Spring Boot project, Spring Boot auto-configuration automatically tries to configure the beans based on the dependency.

For example, when we add a dependency in `spring-boot-starter-web`, the following beans are auto-configured:

- `basicErrorController`, `handlerExceptionResolver`: It is the basic exception handling. It shows a default error page when an exception occurs.
- `beanNameHandlerMapping`: It is used to resolve paths to a handler (controller).
- `characterEncodingFilter`: It provides default character encoding UTF-8.
- `dispatcherServlet`: It is the front controller in Spring MVC applications.
- `jacksonObjectMapper`: It translates objects to JSON and JSON to objects in REST services.
- `messageConverters`: It is the default message converters to convert from objects into XML or JSON and vice versa.
- `multipartResolver`: It provides support to upload files in web applications.
- `mvcValidator`: It supports validation of HTTP requests.
- `viewResolver`: It resolves a logical view name to a physical view.
- `propertySourcesPlaceholderConfigurer`: It supports the externalization of application configuration.
- `requestContextFilter`: It defaults the filter for requests.

- **restTemplateBuilder**: It is used to make calls to REST services.
- **tomcatEmbeddedServletContainerFactory**: Tomcat is the default embedded servlet container for Spring Boot-based web applications.

In the next section, let's look at some of the starter projects and the auto-configuration they provide.

Starter Projects

The following table shows some of the important starter projects provided by Spring Boot:

Starter	Description
spring-boot-starter-web-services	This is a starter project to develop XML-based web services.
spring-boot-starter-web	This is a starter project to build Spring MVC-based web applications or RESTful applications. It uses Tomcat as the default embedded servlet container.
spring-boot-starter-activemq	This supports message-based communication using JMS on ActiveMQ.
spring-boot-starter-integration	This supports the Spring Integration Framework that provides implementations for Enterprise Integration Patterns.
spring-boot-starter-test	This provides support for various unit testing frameworks, such as JUnit, Mockito, and Hamcrest matchers.
spring-boot-starter-jdbc	This provides support for using Spring JDBC. It configures a Tomcat JDBC connection pool by default.

Starter	Description
`spring-boot-starter-validation`	This provides support for the Java Bean Validation API. Its default implementation is hibernate-validator.
`spring-boot-starter-hateoas`	HATEOAS stands for Hypermedia as the Engine of Application State. RESTful services that use HATEOAS return links to additional resources that are related to the current context in addition to data.
`spring-boot-starter-jersey`	JAX-RS is the Java EE standard to develop REST APIs. Jersey is the default implementation. This starter project provides support to build JAX-RS-based REST APIs.
`spring-boot-starter-websocket`	HTTP is stateless. WebSockets allow you to maintain a connection between the server and the browser. This starter project provides support for Spring WebSockets.
`spring-boot-starter-aop`	This provides support for Aspect Oriented Programming. It also provides support for AspectJ for advanced aspect-oriented programming.
`spring-boot-starter-amqp`	With RabbitMQ as the default, this starter project provides message passing with AMQP.
`spring-boot-starter-security`	This starter project enables auto-configuration for Spring Security.
`spring-boot-starter-data-jpa`	This provides support for Spring Data JPA. Its default implementation is Hibernate.

Starter	Description
`spring-boot-starter`	This is a base starter for Spring Boot applications. It provides support for auto-configuration and logging.
`spring-boot-starter-batch`	This provides support to develop batch applications using Spring Batch.
`spring-boot-starter-cache`	This is the basic support for caching using Spring Framework.
`spring-boot-starter-data-rest`	This is the support to expose REST services using Spring Data REST.

Until now, we have set up a basic web application and understood some of the important concepts related to Spring Boot:

- Auto-configuration
- Starter projects
- `spring-boot-maven-plugin`
- `spring-boot-starter-parent`
- Annotation `@SpringBootApplication`

Now let's shift our focus to understanding what REST is and building a REST Service.

What is REST?

Representational State Transfer (REST) is basically an architectural style for the web. REST specifies a set of constraints. These constraints ensure that clients (service consumers and browsers) can interact with servers in flexible ways.

Let's first understand some common terminologies:

- **Server**: Service provider. Exposes services which can be consumed by clients.
- **Client**: Service consumer. Could be a browser or another system.
- **Resource**: Any information can be a resource: a person, an image, a video, or a product you want to sell.
- **Representation**: A specific way a resource can be represented. For example, the product resource can be represented using JSON, XML, or HTML. Different clients might request different representations of the resource.

Some of the important REST constraints are listed as follows:

- **Client-Server**: There should be a server (service provider) and a client (service consumer). This enables loose coupling and independent evolution of the server and client as new technologies emerge.
- **Stateless**: Each service should be stateless. Subsequent requests should not depend on some data from a previous request being temporarily stored. Messages should be self-descriptive.
- **Uniform interface**: Each resource has a resource identifier. In the case of web services, we use this URI example: `/users/Jack/todos/1`. In this, URI Jack is the name of the user. `1` is the ID of the todo we would want to retrieve.
- **Cacheable**: The service response should be cacheable. Each response should indicate whether it is cacheable.
- **Layered system**: The consumer of the service should not assume a direct connection to the service provider. Since requests can be cached, the client might be getting the cached response from a middle layer.
- **Manipulation of resources through representations**: A resource can have multiple representations. It should be possible to modify the resource through a message with any of these representations.
- **Hypermedia as the engine of application state (HATEOAS)**: The consumer of a RESTful application should know about only one fixed service URL. All subsequent resources should be discoverable from the links included in the resource representations.

An example response with the HATEOAS link is shown here. This is the response to a request to retrieve all todos:

```
    {
"_embedded":{
"todos":[
{
```

```
"user":"Jill",
"desc":"Learn Hibernate",
"done":false,
"_links":{
"self":{
"href":"http://localhost:8080/todos/1"
                    },
"todo":{
"href":"http://localhost:8080/todos/1"
}
}
}
]
},
"_links":{
"self":{
"href":"http://localhost:8080/todos"
},
"profile":{
"href":"http://localhost:8080/profile/todos"
},
"search":{
"href":"http://localhost:8080/todos/search"
}
}
}
```

The preceding response includes links to the following:

- Specific todos (`http://localhost:8080/todos/1`)
- Search resource (`http://localhost:8080/todos/search`)

If the service consumer wants to do a search, it has the option of taking the search URL from the response and sending the search request to it. This would reduce coupling between the service provider and the service consumer.

The initial services we develop will not be adhering to all these constraints. As we move on to the next lessons, we will introduce you to the details of these constraints and add them to the services to make them more RESTful.

First REST Service

Let's start with creating a simple REST service returning a welcome message. We will create a simple POJO `WelcomeBean` class with a member field called message and one argument constructor, as shown in the following code snippet:

```
package com.mastering.spring.springboot.bean;

public class WelcomeBean {
  private String message;

  public WelcomeBean(String message) {
    super();
    this.message = message;
  }

  public String getMessage() {
    return message;
  }
}
```

Simple Method Returning String

Let's start with creating a simple REST Controller method returning a string:

```
@RestController
public class BasicController {
  @GetMapping("/welcome")
  public String welcome() {
    return "Hello World";
  }
}
```

A few important things to note are as follows:

- `@RestController`: The `@RestController` annotation provides a combination of `@ResponseBody` and `@Controller` annotations. This is typically used to create REST Controllers.

- `@GetMapping("welcome")`: `@GetMapping` is a shortcut for `@RequestMapping(method = RequestMethod.GET)`. This annotation is a readable alternative. The method with this annotation would handle a Get request to the `welcome` URI.

If we run `Application.java` as a Java application, it would start up the embedded Tomcat container. We can launch up the URL in the browser, as shown in the following screenshot:

Unit Testing

Let's quickly write a unit test to test the preceding `controller` method:

```java
@RunWith(SpringRunner.class)
@WebMvcTest(BasicController.class)
public class BasicControllerTest {

    @Autowired
    private MockMvc mvc;

    @Test
    public void welcome() throws Exception {
      mvc.perform(
      MockMvcRequestBuilders.get("/welcome")
      .accept(MediaType.APPLICATION_JSON))
      .andExpect(status().isOk())
      .andExpect(content().string(
      equalTo("Hello World")));
    }
}
```

In the preceding unit test, we will launch up a Mock MVC instance with `BasicController`. A few quick things to note are as follows:

- `@RunWith(SpringRunner.class)`: SpringRunner is a shortcut to the `SpringJUnit4ClassRunner` annotation. This launches up a simple Spring context for unit testing.

- `@WebMvcTest(BasicController.class)`: This annotation can be used along with SpringRunner to write simple tests for Spring MVC controllers. This will load only the beans annotated with Spring-MVC-related annotations. In this example, we are launching a Web MVC Test context with the class under test being BasicController.

- `@Autowired private MockMvc mvc`: Autowires the MockMvc bean that can be used to make requests.

- `mvc.perform(MockMvcRequestBuilders.get("/welcome").accept(MediaType.APPLICATION_JSON))`: Performs a request to `/welcome` with the `Accept` header value `application/json`.

- `andExpect(status().isOk())`: Expects that the status of the response is 200 (success).

- `andExpect(content().string(equalTo("Hello World")))`: Expects that the content of the response is equal to `"Hello World"`.

Integration Testing

When we do integration testing, we would want to launch the embedded server with all the controllers and beans that are configured. This code snippet shows how we can create a simple integration test:

```java
@RunWith(SpringRunner.class)
@SpringBootTest(classes = Application.class,
webEnvironment = SpringBootTest.WebEnvironment.RANDOM_PORT)
public class BasicControllerIT {

  private static final String LOCAL_HOST =
  "http://localhost:";

  @LocalServerPort
  private int port;

  private TestRestTemplate template = new TestRestTemplate();

  @Test
  public void welcome() throws Exception {
    ResponseEntity<String> response = template
    .getForEntity(createURL("/welcome"), String.class);
    assertThat(response.getBody(), equalTo("Hello World"));
  }

  private String createURL(String uri) {
    return LOCAL_HOST + port + uri;
  }
}
```

A few important things to note are as follows:

- `@SpringBootTest(classes = Application.class, webEnvironment = SpringBootTest.WebEnvironment.RANDOM_PORT)`: It provides additional functionality on top of the Spring `TestContext`. Provides support to configure the port for fully running the container and `TestRestTemplate` (to execute requests).

- `@LocalServerPort private int port`: The `SpringBootTest` would ensure that the port on which the container is running is autowired into the `port` variable.

- `private String createURL(String uri)`: The method to append the local host URL and port to the URI to create a full URL.

- `private TestRestTemplate template = new TestRestTemplate()`: The `TestRestTemplate` is typically used in integration tests. It provides additional functionality on top of `RestTemplate`, which is especially useful in the integration test context. It does not follow redirects so that we can assert response location.

- `template.getForEntity(createURL("/welcome"), String.class)`: It executes a get request for the given URI.

- `assertThat(response.getBody(), equalTo("Hello World"))`: It asserts that the response body content is `"Hello World"`.

Simple REST Method Returning an Object

In the previous method, we returned a string. Let's create a method that returns a proper JSON response. Take a look at the following method:

```
@GetMapping("/welcome-with-object")
public WelcomeBean welcomeWithObject() {
    return new WelcomeBean("Hello World");
}
```

This preceding method returns a simple `WelcomeBean` initialized with a message: `"Hello World"`.

Executing a Request

Let's send a test request and see what response we get. The following screenshot shows the output:

The response for the `http://localhost:8080/welcome-with-object` URL is shown as follows:

```
{"message":"Hello World"}
```

The question that needs to be answered is this: how does the `WelcomeBean` object that we returned get converted into JSON?

Again, it's the magic of Spring Boot auto-configuration. If Jackson is on the classpath of an application, instances of the default object to JSON (and vice versa) converters are auto-configured by Spring Boot.

Unit Testing

Let's quickly write a unit test checking for the JSON response. Let's add the test to `BasicControllerTest`:

```
@Test
public void welcomeWithObject() throws Exception {
  mvc.perform(
    MockMvcRequestBuilders.get("/welcome-with-object")
   .accept(MediaType.APPLICATION_JSON))
   .andExpect(status().isOk())
   .andExpect(content().string(containsString("Hello World")));
}
```

This test is very similar to the earlier unit test except that we are using `containsString` to check whether the content contains a substring `"Hello World"`. We will learn how to write proper JSON tests a little later.

Integration Testing

Let's shift our focus to writing an integration test. Let's add a method to `BasicControllerIT`, as shown in the following code snippet:

```
@Test
public void welcomeWithObject() throws Exception {
  ResponseEntity<String> response =
  template.getForEntity(createURL("/welcome-with-object"),
  String.class);
  assertThat(response.getBody(),
  containsString("Hello World"));
}
```

This method is similar to the earlier integration test except that we are asserting for a sub-string using the `String`method.

Get Method with Path Variables

Let's shift our attention to path variables. Path variables are used to bind values from the URI to a variable on the controller method. In the following example, we want to parameterize the name so that we can customize the welcome message with a name:

```
private static final String helloWorldTemplate = "Hello World,
%s!";

@GetMapping("/welcome-with-parameter/name/{name}")
public WelcomeBean welcomeWithParameter(@PathVariable String name)
  {
      return new WelcomeBean(String.format(helloWorldTemplate,
name));
  }
```

A few important things to note are as follows:

- `@GetMapping("/welcome-with-parameter/name/{name}")`: {name} indicates that this value will be the variable. We can have multiple variable templates in a URI.

- `welcomeWithParameter(@PathVariable String name)`: @PathVariable ensures that the variable value from the URI is bound to the variable name.

- `String.format(helloWorldTemplate, name)`: A simple string format to replace %s in the template with the name.

Executing a Request

Let's send a test request and see what response we get. The following screenshot shows the response:

The response for the `http://localhost:8080/welcome-with-parameter/name/Buddy` URL is as follows:

```
{"message":"Hello World, Buddy!"}
```

As expected, the name in the URI is used to form the message in the response.

Unit Testing

Let's quickly write a unit test for the preceding method. We would want to pass a name as part of the URI and check whether the response contains the name. The following code shows how we can do that:

```
@Test
public void welcomeWithParameter() throws Exception {
  mvc.perform(
  MockMvcRequestBuilders.get("/welcome-with-parameter/name/Buddy")
  .accept(MediaType.APPLICATION_JSON))
  .andExpect(status().isOk())
  .andExpect(
  content().string(containsString("Hello World, Buddy")));
}
```

A few important things to note are as follows:

- `MockMvcRequestBuilders.get("/welcome-with-parameter/name/Buddy")`: This matches against the variable template in the URI. We pass in the name `Buddy`.
- `.andExpect(content().string(containsString("Hello World, Buddy")))`: We expect the response to contain the message with the name.

Integration Testing

The integration test for the preceding method is very simple. Take a look at the following `test` method:

```
@Test
public void welcomeWithParameter() throws Exception {
  ResponseEntity<String> response =
  template.getForEntity(
  createURL("/welcome-with-parameter/name/Buddy"), String.class);
  assertThat(response.getBody(),
  containsString("Hello World, Buddy"));
}
```

A few important things to note are as follows:

- `createURL("/welcome-with-parameter/name/Buddy")`: This matches against the variable template in the URI. We are passing in the name, Buddy.
- `assertThat(response.getBody(), containsString("Hello World, Buddy"))`: We expect the response to contain the message with the name.

In this section, we looked at the basics of creating a simple REST service with Spring Boot. We also ensured that we have good unit tests and integration tests. While these are really basic, they lay the foundation for more complex REST services we will build in the next section.

The unit tests and integration tests we implemented can have better asserts using a JSON comparison instead of a simple substring comparison. We will focus on it in the tests we write for the REST services we will create in the next sections.

Creating a Todo Resource

We will focus on creating REST services for a basic todo management system. We will create services for the following:

- Retrieving a list of todos for a given user
- Retrieving details for a specific todo
- Creating a todo for a user

Request Methods, Operations, and Uris

One of the best practices of REST services is to use the appropriate HTTP request method based on the action we perform. In the services we exposed until now, we used the GET method, as we focused on services that read data.

The following table shows the appropriate HTTP Request method based on the operation that we perform:

HTTP Request Method	Operation
GET	Read--Retrieve details for a resource
POST	Create--Create a new item or resource
PUT	Update/replace
PATCH	Update/modify a part of the resource
DELETE	Delete

Let's quickly map the services that we want to create to the appropriate request methods:

- **Retrieving a list of todos for a given user**: This is READ. We will use GET. We will use a URI: /users/{name}/todos. One more good practice is to use plurals for static things in the URI: users, todo, and so on. This results in more readable URIs.

- **Retrieving details for a specific todo**: Again, we will use GET. We will use a URI /users/{name}/todos/{id}. You can see that this is consistent with the earlier URI that we decided for the list of todos.

- **Creating a todo for a user**: For the create operation, the suggested HTTP Request method is POST. To create a new todo, we will post to URI /users/{name}/todos.

Beans and Services

To be able to retrieve and store details of a todo, we need a Todo bean and a service to retrieve and store the details.

Let's create a Todo Bean:

```
public class Todo {
  private int id;
  private String user;

  private String desc;
```

```
    private Date targetDate;
    private boolean isDone;

    public Todo() {}

    public Todo(int id, String user, String desc,
    Date targetDate, boolean isDone) {
      super();
      this.id = id;
      this.user = user;
      this.desc = desc;
      this.targetDate = targetDate;
      this.isDone = isDone;
    }

    //ALL Getters
}
```

We have a created a simple Todo bean with the ID, the name of user, the description of the todo, the todo target date, and an indicator for the completion status. We added a constructor and getters for all fields.

Let's add `TodoService` now:

```
@Service
public class TodoService {
  private static List<Todo> todos = new ArrayList<Todo>();
  private static int todoCount = 3;

  static {
    todos.add(new Todo(1, "Jack", "Learn Spring MVC",
    new Date(), false));
    todos.add(new Todo(2, "Jack", "Learn Struts", new Date(),
    false));
    todos.add(new Todo(3, "Jill", "Learn Hibernate", new Date(),
    false));
  }

  public List<Todo> retrieveTodos(String user) {
    List<Todo> filteredTodos = new ArrayList<Todo>();
    for (Todo todo : todos) {
      if (todo.getUser().equals(user))
      filteredTodos.add(todo);
    }
    return filteredTodos;
```

```
  }

  public Todo addTodo(String name, String desc,
  Date targetDate, boolean isDone) {
    Todo todo = new Todo(++todoCount, name, desc, targetDate,
    isDone);
    todos.add(todo);
    return todo;
  }

  public Todo retrieveTodo(int id) {
    for (Todo todo : todos) {
    if (todo.getId() == id)
      return todo;
    }
    return null;
  }
}
```

Quick things to note are as follows:

- To keep things simple, this service does not talk to the database. It maintains an in-memory array list of todos. This list is initialized using a static initializer.

- We are exposing a couple of simple retrieve methods and a method to add a to-do.

Now that we have the service and bean ready, we can create our first service to retrieve a list of to-do's for a user.

Retrieving a Todo List

We will create a new RestController annotation called TodoController. The code for the retrieve todos method is shown as follows:

```
@RestController
public class TodoController {
 @Autowired
 private TodoService todoService;

 @GetMapping("/users/{name}/todos")
 public List<Todo> retrieveTodos(@PathVariable String name) {
    return todoService.retrieveTodos(name);
 }
}
```

A couple of things to note are as follows:

- We are autowiring the todo service using the `@Autowired` annotation
- We use the `@GetMapping` annotation to map the Get request for the `"/users/{name}/todos"` URI to the `retrieveTodos` method

Executing the Service

Let's send a test request and see what response we get. The following screenshot shows the output:

```
localhost:8080/users/Jack/todos

[{"id":1,"user":"Jack","desc":"Learn Spring
MVC","targetDate":1481607268779,"done":false},
{"id":2,"user":"Jack","desc":"Learn
Struts","targetDate":1481607268779,"done":false}]
```

The response for the `http://localhost:8080/users/Jack/todos` URL is as follows:

```
[
 {"id":1,"user":"Jack","desc":"Learn Spring
  MVC","targetDate":1481607268779,"done":false},
 {"id":2,"user":"Jack","desc":"Learn
  Struts","targetDate":1481607268779, "done":false}
]
```

Unit Testing

The code to unit test the `TodoController` class is shown in the following screenshot:

```
@RunWith(SpringRunner.class)
@WebMvcTest(TodoController.class)
public class TodoControllerTest {

 @Autowired
 private MockMvc mvc;

 @MockBean
 private TodoService service;

 @Test
```

```
public void retrieveTodos() throws Exception {
 List<Todo> mockList = Arrays.asList(new Todo(1, "Jack",
 "Learn Spring MVC", new Date(), false), new Todo(2, "Jack",
 "Learn Struts", new Date(), false));

 when(service.retrieveTodos(anyString())).thenReturn(mockList);

 MvcResult result = mvc
 .perform(MockMvcRequestBuilders.get("/users
 /Jack/todos").accept(MediaType.APPLICATION_JSON))
 .andExpect(status().isOk()).andReturn();

 String expected = "["
 + "{id:1,user:Jack,desc:\"Learn Spring MVC\",done:false}" +","
 + "{id:2,user:Jack,desc:\"Learn Struts\",done:false}" + "]";

 JSONAssert.assertEquals(expected, result.getResponse()
  .getContentAsString(), false);
 }
}
```

A few important things to note are as follows:

- We are writing a unit test. So, we want to test only the logic present in the `TodoController` class. So, we initialize a Mock MVC framework with only the `TodoController` class using `@WebMvcTest(TodoController.class)`.

- `@MockBean private TodoService service`: We are mocking out the `TodoService` using the `@MockBean`annotation. In test classes that are run with `SpringRunner`, the beans defined with `@MockBean` will be replaced by a mock, created using the Mockito framework.

- `when(service.retrieveTodos(anyString())).thenReturn(mockList)`: We are mocking the `retrieveTodos` service method to return the mock list.

- `MvcResult result = ..`: We are accepting the result of the request into an MvcResult variable to enable us to perform assertions on the response.

- `JSONAssert.assertEquals(expected, result.getResponse().getContentAsString(), false)`: JSONAssert is a very useful framework to perform asserts on JSON. It compares the response text with the expected value. `JSONAssert` is intelligent enough to ignore values that are not specified. Another advantage is a clear failure message in case of assertion failures. The last parameter, false, indicates using non-strict mode. If it is changed to true, then the expected should exactly match the result.

Integration Testing

The code to perform integration testing on the `TodoController` class is shown in the following code snippet. It launches up the entire Spring context with all the controllers and beans defined:

```
@RunWith(SpringJUnit4ClassRunner.class)
@SpringBootTest(classes = Application.class, webEnvironment =
SpringBootTest.WebEnvironment.RANDOM_PORT)
public class TodoControllerIT {

 @LocalServerPort
 private int port;

 private TestRestTemplate template = new TestRestTemplate();

 @Test
 public void retrieveTodos() throws Exception {
  String expected = "["
  + "{id:1,user:Jack,desc:\"Learn Spring MVC\",done:false}" + ","
  + "{id:2,user:Jack,desc:\"Learn Struts\",done:false}" + "]";

  String uri = "/users/Jack/todos";

  ResponseEntity<String> response =
  template.getForEntity(createUrl(uri), String.class);

  JSONAssert.assertEquals(expected, response.getBody(), false);
 }

 private String createUrl(String uri) {
 return "http://localhost:" + port + uri;
 }
}
```

This test is very similar to the integration test for `BasicController`, except that we are using `JSONAssert` to assert the response.

Retrieving Details for a Specific Todo

We will now add the method to retrieve details for a specific Todo:

```
@GetMapping(path = "/users/{name}/todos/{id}")
public Todo retrieveTodo(@PathVariable String name, @PathVariable
int id) {
   return todoService.retrieveTodo(id);
}
```

A couple of things to note are as follows:

- The URI mapped is `/users/{name}/todos/{id}`
- We have two path variables defined for `name` and `id`

Executing the Service

Let's send a test request and see what response we will get, as shown in the following screenshot:

```
←    localhost:8080/users/Jack/todos/1                                    ⟳

{"id":1,"user":"Jack","desc":"Learn Spring
MVC","targetDate":1481607268779,"done":false}
```

The response for the `http://localhost:8080/users/Jack/todos/1` URL is shown as follows:

```
{"id":1,"user":"Jack","desc":"Learn Spring MVC",
"targetDate":1481607268779,"done":false}
```

Unit Testing

The code to unit test `retrieveTodo` is as follows:

```
@Test
public void retrieveTodo() throws Exception {
    Todo mockTodo = new Todo(1, "Jack", "Learn Spring MVC",
    new Date(), false);

    when(service.retrieveTodo(anyInt())).thenReturn(mockTodo);

    MvcResult result = mvc.perform(
    MockMvcRequestBuilders.get("/users/Jack/todos/1")
    .accept(MediaType.APPLICATION_JSON))
    .andExpect(status().isOk()).andReturn();

    String expected = "{id:1,user:Jack,desc:\"Learn Spring
    MVC\",done:false}";

  JSONAssert.assertEquals(expected,
    result.getResponse().getContentAsString(), false);

}
```

A few important things to note are as follows:

- `when(service.retrieveTodo(anyInt())).thenReturn(mockTodo)`: We are mocking the `retrieveTodo` service method to return the mock todo.

- `MvcResult result = ..`: We are accepting the result of the request into an MvcResult variable to enable us to perform assertions on the response.

- `JSONAssert.assertEquals(expected, result.getResponse().getContentAsString(), false)`: Asserts whether the result is as expected.

Integration Testing

The code to perform integration testing on `retrieveTodos` in `TodoController` is shown in the following code snippet. This would be added to the `TodoControllerIT` class:

```
@Test
public void retrieveTodo() throws Exception {
  String expected = "{id:1,user:Jack,desc:\"Learn Spring
  MVC\",done:false}";
  ResponseEntity<String> response = template.getForEntity(
  createUrl("/users/Jack/todos/1"), String.class);
  JSONAssert.assertEquals(expected, response.getBody(), false);
}
```

Adding A Todo

We will now add the method to create a new Todo. The HTTP method to be used for creation is `Post`. We will post to a `"/users/{name}/todos"` URI:

```
@PostMapping("/users/{name}/todos")
ResponseEntity<?> add(@PathVariable String name,
@RequestBody Todo todo) {
  Todo createdTodo = todoService.addTodo(name, todo.getDesc(),
  todo.getTargetDate(), todo.isDone());
  if (createdTodo == null) {
    return ResponseEntity.noContent().build();
  }

  URI location = ServletUriComponentsBuilder.fromCurrentRequest()

  .path("/{id}").buildAndExpand(createdTodo.getId()).toUri();
  return ResponseEntity.created(location).build();
}
```

A few things to note are as follows:

- `@PostMapping("/users/{name}/todos")`: `@PostMapping` annotations map the `add()` method to the HTTP Request with a `POST` method.

- `ResponseEntity<?> add(@PathVariable String name, @RequestBody Todo todo)`: An HTTP post request should ideally return the URI to the created resources. We use `ResourceEntity` to do this. `@RequestBody` binds the body of the request directly to the bean.

- `ResponseEntity.noContent().build()`: Used to return that the creation of the resource failed.

- `ServletUriComponentsBuilder.fromCurrentRequest().path("/{id}").buildAndExpand(createdTodo.getId()).toUri()`: Forms the URI for the created resource that can be returned in the response.

- `ResponseEntity.created(location).build()`: Returns a status of `201(CREATED)` with a link to the resource created.

Postman

If you are on Mac, you might want to try the Paw application as well.

Let's send a test request and see what response we get. The following screenshot shows the response:

We will use Postman app to interact with the REST Services. You can install it from the website, `https://www.getpostman.com/`. It is available on Windows and Mac. A Google Chrome plugin is also available.

Executing the POST Service

To create a new Todo using `POST`, we would need to include the JSON for the Todo in the body of the request. The following screenshot shows how we can use the Postman app to create the request and the response after executing the request:

A few important things to note are as follows:

- We are sending a POST request. So, we choose the `POST` from the top-left dropdown.

- To send the Todo JSON as part of the body of the request, we select the `raw` option in the `Body` tab (highlighted with a blue dot). We choose the content type as JSON (`application/json`).

- Once the request is successfully executed, you can see the status of the request in the bar in the middle of the screen: `Status: 201 Created`.

- The location is `http://localhost:8080/users/Jack/todos/5`. This is the URI of the newly created todo that is received in the response.

Complete details of the request to `http://localhost:8080/users/Jack/todos` are shown in the block, as follows:

```
Header
Content-Type:application/json

Body
 {
   "user": "Jack",
   "desc": "Learn Spring Boot",
    "done": false
  }
```

Unit Testing

The code to unit test the created Todo is shown as follows:

```
@Test
public void createTodo() throws Exception {
 Todo mockTodo = new Todo(CREATED_TODO_ID, "Jack",
 "Learn Spring MVC", new Date(), false);
  String todo = "{"user":"Jack","desc":"Learn Spring MVC",
  "done":false}";

 when(service.addTodo(anyString(), anyString(),
 isNull(),anyBoolean()))
 .thenReturn(mockTodo);

mvc
 .perform(MockMvcRequestBuilders.post("/users/Jack/todos")
 .content(todo)
 .contentType(MediaType.APPLICATION_JSON)
 )
 .andExpect(status().isCreated())
 .andExpect(
   header().string("location",containsString("/users/Jack/todos/"
  + CREATED_TODO_ID)));
}
```

A few important things to note are as follows:

* `String todo = "{"user":"Jack","desc":"Learn Spring MVC","done":false}"`: The Todo content to post to the create todo service.

- `when(service.addTodo(anyString(), anyString(), isNull(), anyBoolean())).thenReturn(mockTodo)`: Mocks the service to return a dummy todo.
- `MockMvcRequestBuilders.post("/users/Jack/todos").content(todo).contentType(MediaType.APPLICATION_JSON))`: Creates a POST to a given URI with the given content type.
- `andExpect(status().isCreated())`: Expects that the status is created.
- `andExpect(header().string("location",containsString("/users/Jack/todos/" + CREATED_TODO_ID)))`: Expects that the header contains `location` with the URI of created resource.

Integration Testing

The code to perform integration testing on the created todo in `TodoController` is shown as follows. This would be added to the `TodoControllerIT` class, as follows:

```
@Test
public void addTodo() throws Exception {
    Todo todo = new Todo(-1, "Jill", "Learn Hibernate", new Date(),
    false);
    URI location = template
    .postForLocation(createUrl("/users/Jill/todos"),todo);
    assertThat(location.getPath(),
    containsString("/users/Jill/todos/4"));
}
```

A few important things to note are as follows:

- `URI location = template.postForLocation(createUrl("/users/Jill/todos"), todo)`: `postForLocation` is a utility method especially useful in tests to create new resources. We are posting the todo to the given URI and getting the location from the header.
- `assertThat(location.getPath(), containsString("/users/Jill/todos/4"))`: Asserts that the location contains the path to the newly created resource.

Spring Initializr

Do you want to auto-generate Spring Boot projects? Do you want to quickly get started with developing your application? Spring Initializr is the answer.

Spring Initializr is hosted at `http://start.spring.io`. The following screenshot shows how the website looks:

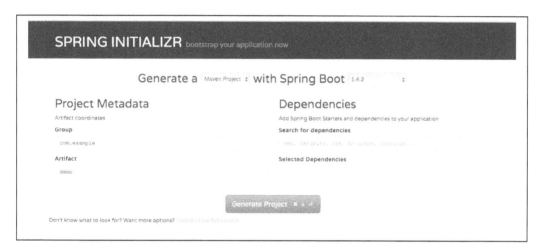

Spring Initializr provides a lot of flexibility in creating projects. You have options to do the following:

- Choose your build tool: Maven or Gradle.
- Choose the Spring Boot version you want to use.
- Configure a `Group ID` and `Artifact ID` for your component.
- Choose the starters (dependencies) that you would want for your project. You can click on the link at the bottom of the screen, `Switch to the full version`, to see all the starter projects you can choose from.
- Choose how to package your component: JAR or WAR.
- Choose the Java version you want to use.
- Choose the JVM language you want to use.

The following screenshot shows some of the options Spring Initializr provides when you expand (click on the link) to the full version:

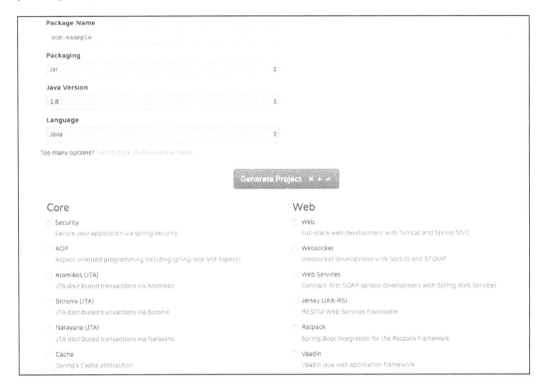

Creating Your First Spring Initializr Project

We will use the full version and enter the values, as follows:

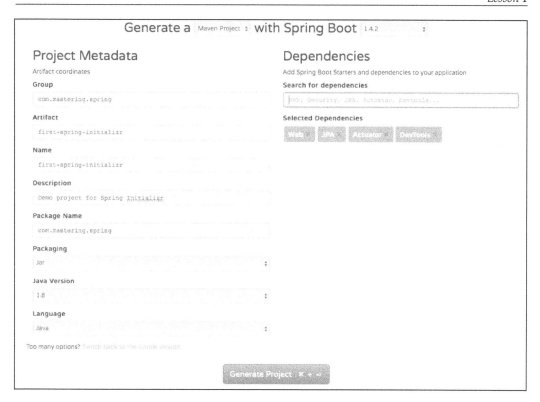

Things to note are as follows:

- `Build tool:` Maven
- `Spring Boot version:` Choose the latest available
- `Group:` com.mastering.spring
- `Artifact:` first-spring-initializr
- `Selected dependencies:` Choose `Web, JPA, Actuator and Dev Tools.` Type in each one of these in the textbox and press *Enter* to choose them. We will learn more about Actuator and Dev Tools in the next section
- `Java version:` 1.8

Go ahead and click on the **Generate Project** button. This will create a `.zip` file and you can download it to your computer.

The following screenshot shows the structure of the project created:

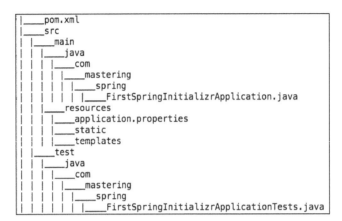

We will now import this project into your IDE. In Eclipse, you can perform the following steps:

1. Launch Eclipse.
2. Navigate to **File | Import**.
3. Choose the existing Maven projects.
4. Browse and select the folder that is the root of the Maven project (the one containing the pom.xml file).
5. Proceed with the defaults and click on **Finish**.

This will import the project into Eclipse. The following screenshot shows the structure of the project in Eclipse:

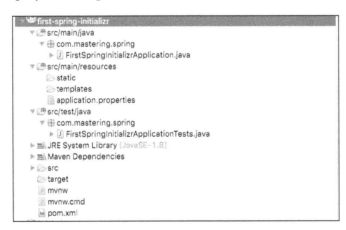

Let's look at some of the important files from the generated project.

pom.xml

The following snippet shows the dependencies that are declared:

```
<dependencies> <dependency> <groupId>org.springframework.boot</
groupId> <artifactId>spring-boot-starter-web</artifactId> </
dependency> <dependency> <groupId>org.springframework.boot</
groupId> <artifactId>spring-boot-starter-data-jpa</artifactId> </
dependency> <dependency> <groupId>org.springframework.boot</
groupId> <artifactId>spring-boot-starter-actuator</artifactId> </
dependency> <dependency> <groupId>org.springframework.boot</groupId>
<artifactId>spring-boot-devtools</artifactId> <scope>runtime</scope>
</dependency> <dependency> <groupId>org.springframework.boot</groupId>
<artifactId>spring-boot-starter-test</artifactId> <scope>test</scope>
</dependency> </dependencies>
```

A few other important observations are as follows:

- The packaging for this component is `.jar`
- `org.springframework.boot:spring-boot-starter-parent` is declared as the parent POM
- `<java.version>1.8</java.version>`: The Java version is 1.8
- Spring Boot Maven Plugin (`org.springframework.boot:spring-boot-maven-plugin`) is configured as a plugin

FirstSpringInitializrApplication.java Class

`FirstSpringInitializrApplication.java` is the launcher for Spring Boot:

```
package com.mastering.spring;
import org.springframework.boot.SpringApplication;
import org.springframework.boot.autoconfigure
.SpringBootApplication;

@SpringBootApplication
public class FirstSpringInitializrApplication {
   public static void main(String[] args) {
     SpringApplication.run(FirstSpringInitializrApplication.class,
     args);
   }
}
```

FirstSpringInitializrApplicationTests Class

FirstSpringInitializrApplicationTests contains the basic context that can be used to start writing the tests as we start developing the application:

```
package com.mastering.spring;
import org.junit.Test;
import org.junit.runner.RunWith;
import org.springframework.boot.test.context.SpringBootTest;
import org.springframework.test.context.junit4.SpringRunner;

@RunWith(SpringRunner.class)
@SpringBootTest
public class FirstSpringInitializrApplicationTests {

  @Test
  public void contextLoads() {
  }
}
```

A Quick Peek into Auto-Configuration

Auto-configuration is one of the most important features of Spring Boot. In this section, we will take a quick peek behind the scenes to understand how Spring Boot auto-configuration works.

Most of the Spring Boot auto-configuration magic comes from spring-boot-autoconfigure-{version}.jar. When we start any Spring Boot applications, a number of beans get auto-configured. How does this happen?

The following screenshot shows an extract from spring.factories from spring-boot-autoconfigure-{version}.jar. We have filtered out some of the configuration in the interest of space:

```
 spring.factories ⊠
31 org.springframework.boot.autoconfigure.data.jpa.JpaRepositoriesAutoConfiguration,\
32 org.springframework.boot.autoconfigure.data.mongo.MongoDataAutoConfiguration,\
33 org.springframework.boot.autoconfigure.data.mongo.MongoRepositoriesAutoConfiguration,\
34 org.springframework.boot.autoconfigure.data.neo4j.Neo4jDataAutoConfiguration,\
35 org.springframework.boot.autoconfigure.data.neo4j.Neo4jRepositoriesAutoConfiguration,\
36 org.springframework.boot.autoconfigure.data.solr.SolrRepositoriesAutoConfiguration,\
37 org.springframework.boot.autoconfigure.data.redis.RedisAutoConfiguration,\
38 org.springframework.boot.autoconfigure.data.redis.RedisRepositoriesAutoConfiguration,\
39 org.springframework.boot.autoconfigure.data.rest.RepositoryRestMvcAutoConfiguration,\
40 org.springframework.boot.autoconfigure.data.web.SpringDataWebAutoConfiguration,\
41 org.springframework.boot.autoconfigure.elasticsearch.jest.JestAutoConfiguration,\
42 org.springframework.boot.autoconfigure.freemarker.FreeMarkerAutoConfiguration,\
43 org.springframework.boot.autoconfigure.gson.GsonAutoConfiguration,\
44 org.springframework.boot.autoconfigure.h2.H2ConsoleAutoConfiguration,\
45 org.springframework.boot.autoconfigure.hateoas.HypermediaAutoConfiguration,\
46 org.springframework.boot.autoconfigure.hazelcast.HazelcastAutoConfiguration,\
47 org.springframework.boot.autoconfigure.hazelcast.HazelcastJpaDependencyAutoConfiguration,\
48 org.springframework.boot.autoconfigure.info.ProjectInfoAutoConfiguration,\
49 org.springframework.boot.autoconfigure.integration.IntegrationAutoConfiguration,\
50 org.springframework.boot.autoconfigure.jackson.JacksonAutoConfiguration,\
51 org.springframework.boot.autoconfigure.jdbc.DataSourceAutoConfiguration,\
52 org.springframework.boot.autoconfigure.jdbc.JdbcTemplateAutoConfiguration,\
53 org.springframework.boot.autoconfigure.jdbc.JndiDataSourceAutoConfiguration,\
54 org.springframework.boot.autoconfigure.jdbc.XADataSourceAutoConfiguration,\
55 org.springframework.boot.autoconfigure.jdbc.DataSourceTransactionManagerAutoConfiguration,\
56 org.springframework.boot.autoconfigure.jms.JmsAutoConfiguration,\
57 org.springframework.boot.autoconfigure.jmx.JmxAutoConfiguration,\
58 org.springframework.boot.autoconfigure.jms.JndiConnectionFactoryAutoConfiguration,\
59 org.springframework.boot.autoconfigure.jms.activemq.ActiveMQAutoConfiguration,\
60 org.springframework.boot.autoconfigure.jms.artemis.ArtemisAutoConfiguration,\
61 org.springframework.boot.autoconfigure.jms.hornetq.HornetQAutoConfiguration,\
62 org.springframework.boot.autoconfigure.flyway.FlywayAutoConfiguration,\
```

The preceding list of auto-configuration classes is run whenever a Spring Boot application is launched. Let's take a quick look at one of them:

`org.springframework.boot.autoconfigure.web.WebMvcAutoConfiguration.`

Here's a small snippet:

```
@Configuration
@ConditionalOnWebApplication
@ConditionalOnClass({ Servlet.class, DispatcherServlet.class,
WebMvcConfigurerAdapter.class })
@ConditionalOnMissingBean(WebMvcConfigurationSupport.class)
@AutoConfigureOrder(Ordered.HIGHEST_PRECEDENCE + 10)
@AutoConfigureAfter(DispatcherServletAutoConfiguration.class)
public class WebMvcAutoConfiguration {
```

Some of the important points to note are as follows:

- `@ConditionalOnClass({ Servlet.class, DispatcherServlet.class, WebMvcConfigurerAdapter.class })`: This auto-configuration is enabled if any of the mentioned classes are in the classpath. When we add a web starter project, we bring in dependencies with all these classes. Hence, this auto-configuration will be enabled.

- `@ConditionalOnMissingBean(WebMvcConfigurationSupport.class)`: This auto-configuration is enabled only if the application does not explicitly declare a bean of the `WebMvcConfigurationSupport.class` class.

- `@AutoConfigureOrder(Ordered.HIGHEST_PRECEDENCE + 10)`: This specifies the precedence of this specific auto-configuration.

Let's look at another small snippet showing one of the methods from the same class:

```
@Bean
@ConditionalOnBean(ViewResolver.class)
@ConditionalOnMissingBean(name = "viewResolver",
value = ContentNegotiatingViewResolver.class)
public ContentNegotiatingViewResolver
viewResolver(BeanFactory beanFactory) {
  ContentNegotiatingViewResolver resolver = new
  ContentNegotiatingViewResolver();
  resolver.setContentNegotiationManager
  (beanFactory.getBean(ContentNegotiationManager.class));
  resolver.setOrder(Ordered.HIGHEST_PRECEDENCE);
  return resolver;
}
```

View resolvers are one of the beans configured by `WebMvcAutoConfiguration` class. The preceding snippet ensures that if a view resolver is not provided by the application, then Spring Boot auto-configures a default view resolver. Here are a few important points to note:

- `@ConditionalOnBean(ViewResolver.class)`: Create this bean if `ViewResolver.class` is on the classpath

- `@ConditionalOnMissingBean(name = "viewResolver", value = ContentNegotiatingViewResolver.class)`: Create this bean if there are no explicitly declared beans of the name `viewResolver` and of type `ContentNegotiatingViewResolver.class`

- The rest of the method is configured in the view resolver

To summarize, all the auto-configuration logic is executed at the start of a Spring Boot application. If a specific class (from a specific dependency or starter project) is available on the classpath, then the auto configuration classes are executed. These auto-configuration classes look at what beans are already configured. Based on the existing beans, they enable the creation of the default beans.

Summary

Spring Boot makes the development of Spring-based applications easy. It enables us to create production-ready applications from day one of a project.

In this lesson, we covered the basics of Spring Boot and REST services. We discussed the different features of Spring Boot and created a few REST services with great tests. We understood what happens in the background with an in-depth look at auto-configuration.

In the next lesson, we will shift our attention toward adding more features to the REST services.

Assessments

1. The _____ class can be used to bootstrap and launch a Spring application from a Java main method.

2. Which of the following methods is used to append the local host URL and port to the URI to create a full URL?

    1. Private URL(String uri)
    2. private String create(String uri)
    3. private String CreateURL(String uri)
    4. private String createURL(String uri)

3. State whether True or False: Tomcat server is launched on port 8080--Tomcat started on port(s): 8080 (http).

4. Which of the following starter templates provides support for various unit testing frameworks such as JUnit, Mockito, and Hamcrest? These frameworks does the work of orchestrating the lock contention in Spring Boot.

   1. spring-boot-starter-test

   2. spring-boot-starter-testframe

   3. spring-boot-starter-unittest

   4. spring-boot-starter-testorchestration

5. State whether True or False: The multipartResolver does not provide support to upload files in web applications.

2
Extending Microservices

We built a basic component offering a few services in Lesson 1, *Building Microservices with Spring Boot*. In this lesson, we will focus on adding more features to make our microservice production ready.

We will discuss how to add these features to our microservice:

- Exception handling
- HATEOAS
- Caching
- Internationalization

We will also discuss how to document our microservice using Swagger. We will look at the basics of securing the microservice with Spring Security.

Exception Handling

Exception handling is one of the important parts of developing web services. When something goes wrong, we would want to return a good description of what went wrong to the service consumer. You would not want the service to crash without returning anything useful to the service consumer.

Spring Boot provides good default exception handling. We will start with looking at the default exception handling features provided by Spring Boot before moving on to customizing them.

Spring Boot Default Exception Handling

To understand the default exception handling provided by Spring Boot, let's start with firing a request to a nonexistent URL.

Non-Existent Resource

Let's send a GET request to `http://localhost:8080/non-existing-resource` using a header (`Content-Type:application/json`).

The following screenshot shows the response when we execute the request:

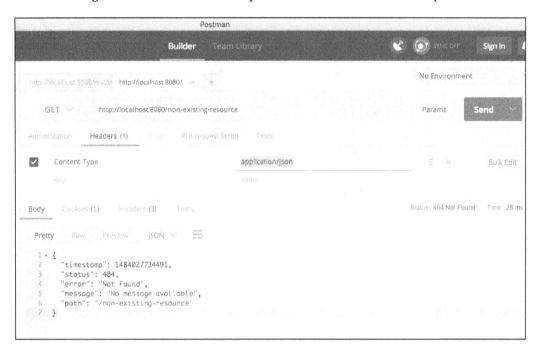

The response is as shown in the following code snippet:

```
{
    "timestamp": 1484027734491,
    "status": 404,
    "error": "Not Found",
    "message": "No message available",
    "path": "/non-existing-resource"
}
```

Some important things to note are as follows:

- The response header has an HTTP status of `404 - Resource Not Found`
- Spring Boot returns a valid JSON message as a response with the message stating that the resource is not found

Resource Throwing an Exception

Let's create a resource that throws an exception, and send a GET request to it in order to understand how the application reacts to runtime exceptions.

Let's create a dummy service that throws an exception. The following code snippet shows a simple service:

```
@GetMapping(path = "/users/dummy-service")
public Todo errorService() {
  throw new RuntimeException("Some Exception Occured");
}
```

Some important things to note are as follows:

We are creating a GET service with the URI /users/dummy-service.

The service throws a RuntimeException. We chose RuntimeException to be able to create the exception easily. We can easily replace it with a custom exception; if needed.

Let's fire a GET request to the preceding service at http://localhost:8080/users/dummy-service using Postman. The response is as shown in the following code:

```
{
  "timestamp": 1484028119553,
  "status": 500,
  "error": "Internal Server Error",
  "exception": "java.lang.RuntimeException",
  "message": "Some Exception Occured",
  "path": "/users/dummy-service"
}
```

Some important things to note are as follows:

- The response header has an HTTP status of 500; Internal server error
- Spring Boot also returns the message with which the exception is thrown

As we can see in the preceding two examples, Spring Boot provides good default exception handling. In the next section, we will focus on understanding how the application reacts to custom exceptions.

Throwing a Custom Exception

Let's create a custom exception and throw it from a service. Take a look at the following code:

```java
public class TodoNotFoundException extends RuntimeException {
  public TodoNotFoundException(String msg) {
    super(msg);
  }
}
```

It's a very simple piece of code that defines `TodoNotFoundException`.

Now let's enhance our `TodoController` class to throw `TodoNotFoundException` when a `todo` with a given ID is not found:

```java
@GetMapping(path = "/users/{name}/todos/{id}")
public Todo retrieveTodo(@PathVariable String name,
@PathVariable int id) {
  Todo todo = todoService.retrieveTodo(id);
  if (todo == null) {
    throw new TodoNotFoundException("Todo Not Found");
   }

 return todo;
}
```

If `todoService` returns a null `todo`, we throw; `TodoNotFoundException`.

When we execute the service with a GET request to a nonexistent: `todo`(`http://localhost:8080/users/Jack/todos/222`), we get the response shown in the following code snippet:

```json
{
  "timestamp": 1484029048788,
  "status": 500,
  "error": "Internal Server Error",
  "exception":
  "com.mastering.spring.springboot.bean.TodoNotFoundException",
  "message": "Todo Not Found",
  "path": "/users/Jack/todos/222"
}
```

As we can see, a clear exception response is sent back to the service consumer. However, there is one thing that can be improved further--the response status. When a resource is not found, it is recommended that you return a 404 - Resource Not Found status. We will look at how to customize the response status in the next example.

Customizing the Exception Message

Let's look at how to customize the preceding exception and return the proper response status with a customized message.

Let's create a bean to define the structure of our custom exception message:

```java
public class ExceptionResponse {
  private Date timestamp = new Date();
  private String message;
  private String details;

  public ExceptionResponse(String message, String details) {
    super();
    this.message = message;
    this.details = details;
  }

  public Date getTimestamp() {
    return timestamp;
  }

  public String getMessage() {
    return message;
  }

  public String getDetails() {
    return details;
  }
}
```

We have created a simple exception response bean with an auto-populated timestamp with a few additional properties namely messages and details.

When; `TodoNotFoundException` is thrown, we would want to return a response using the `ExceptionResponse` bean. The following code shows how we can create a global exception handling for `TodoNotFoundException.class`:

```
@ControllerAdvice
@RestController
public class RestResponseEntityExceptionHandler
  extends  ResponseEntityExceptionHandler
  {
    @ExceptionHandler(TodoNotFoundException.class)
    public final ResponseEntity<ExceptionResponse>
    todoNotFound(TodoNotFoundException ex) {
      ExceptionResponse exceptionResponse =
      new ExceptionResponse(  ex.getMessage(),
      "Any details you would want to add");
      return new ResponseEntity<ExceptionResponse>
      (exceptionResponse, new HttpHeaders(),
      HttpStatus.NOT_FOUND);
    }
  }
```

Some important things to note are as follows:

`RestResponseEntityExceptionHandler extends ResponseEntityExceptionHandler`: We are extending `ResponseEntityExceptionHandler`, which the base class is provided by Spring MVC for centralised exception handling `ControllerAdvice` classes.

`@ExceptionHandler(TodoNotFoundException.class)`: This defines that the method to follow will handle the specific exception `TodoNotFoundException.class`. Any other exceptions for which custom exception handling is not defined will follow the default exception handling provided by Spring Boot.

`ExceptionResponse exceptionResponse = new ExceptionResponse(ex. getMessage(), "Any details you would want to add")`: This creates a custom exception response.

`new ResponseEntity<ExceptionResponse>(exceptionResponse,new HttpHeaders(), HttpStatus.NOT_FOUND)`: This is the definition to return a `404 Resource Not Found` response with the custom exception defined earlier.

When we execute the service with a `GET` request to a nonexistent; todo(`http://localhost:8080/users/Jack/todos/222`), we get the following response:

```
{
  "timestamp": 1484030343311,
  "message": "Todo Not Found",
  "details": "Any details you would want to add"
}
```

If you want to create a generic exception message for all exceptions, we can add a method to `RestResponseEntityExceptionHandler` with the `@ExceptionHandler(Exception.class)` annotation.

The following code snippet shows how we can do this:

```
@ExceptionHandler(Exception.class)
public final ResponseEntity<ExceptionResponse> todoNotFound(
Exception ex) {
    //Customize and return the response
}
```

Any exception for which a custom exception handler is not defined; will be handled by the preceding method.

Response Status

One of the important things to focus on with REST services is the response status of an error response. The following table shows the scenarios and the error response status to use:

Situation	Response Status
The request body does not meet the API specification. It does not contain enough details or contains validation errors.	;400 BAD REQUEST
Authentication or authorization failure.	401 UNAUTHORIZED
The user cannot perform the operation due to various factor, such as exceeding limits.	403 FORBIDDEN
The resource does not exist.	404 NOT FOUND

Situation	Response Status
Unsupported operation, for example, trying POST on a resource where only GET is allowed.	405 METHOD NOT ALLOWED
Error on a server. Ideally, this should not happen. The consumer; would not be able to fix this.	500 INTERNAL SERVER ERROR

In this section, we looked at the default exception handling provided by Spring Boot and how we can customize it further to suit our needs.

HATEOAS

HATEOAS (Hypermedia as the Engine of Application State) is one of the constraints of the REST application architecture.

Let's consider a situation where a service consumer is consuming numerous services from a service provider. The easiest way to develop this kind of system is to have the service consumer store the individual resource URIs of every resource they need from the service provider. However, this would create tight coupling between the service provider and the service consumer. Whenever any of the resource URIs change on the service provider, the service consumer needs to be updated.

Consider a; typical web application. Let's say I navigate to my bank account details page. Almost all banking websites would show links to all the transactions that are possible on my bank account on the screen so that I can easily navigate using the link.

What if we can bring a; similar concept to RESTful services so that a service returns not only the data about the requested resource, but also provides details of other related resources?

HATEOAS brings this concept of displaying related links for a given resource to RESTful services. When we return the details of a specific resource, we also return links to operations that can be performed on the resource, as well as links to related resources. If a service consumer can use the links from the response to perform transactions, then it would not need to hardcode all links.

An extract of constraints related to HATEOAS presented by Roy Fielding (http://roy.gbiv.com/untangled/2008/rest-apis-must-be-hypertext-driven) is as follows:

A REST API must not define fixed resource names or hierarchies (an obvious coupling of client and server). Servers must have the freedom to control their own namespace. Instead, allow servers to instruct clients on how to construct appropriate URIs, such as is done in HTML forms and URI templates, by defining those instructions within media types and link relations.

A REST API should be entered with no prior knowledge beyond the initial URI (bookmark) and set of standardized media types that are appropriate for the intended audience (i.e., expected to be understood by any client that might use the API). From that point on, all application state transitions must be driven by client selection of server-provided choices that are present in the received representations or implied by the user's manipulation of those representations. The transitions may be determined (or limited by) the client's knowledge of media types and resource communication mechanisms, both of which may be improved on-the-fly (e.g., code-on-demand).

An example response with HATEOAS link is shown here. This is the response to the /todos request in order to retrieve all todos:

```
{
  "_embedded" : {
    "todos" : [ {
      "user" : "Jill",
      "desc" : "Learn Hibernate",
      "done" : false,
     "_links" : {
      "self" : {
             "href" : "http://localhost:8080/todos/1"
             },
         "todo" : {
             "href" : "http://localhost:8080/todos/1"
             }
        }
    } ]
  },
  "_links" : {
  "self" : {
         "href" : "http://localhost:8080/todos"
         },
```

```
"profile" : {
        "href" : "http://localhost:8080/profile/todos"
        },
"search" : {
        "href" : "http://localhost:8080/todos/search"
        }
    },
}
```

The preceding response includes links to the following:

- Specific `todos` (`http://localhost:8080/todos/1`)
- Search resource (`http://localhost:8080/todos/search`)

If the service consumer wants to do a search, it has the option of taking the search URL from the response and sending the search request to it. This would reduce coupling between the service provider and the service consumer.

Sending HATEOAS Links in Response

Now that we understand what HATEOAS is, let's look at how we can send links related to a resource in the response.

Spring Boot Starter HATEOAS

Spring Boot has a specific starter for HATEOAS called `spring-boot-starter-hateoas`. We need to add it to the `pom.xml` file.

The following code snippet shows the dependency block:

```
<dependency>
  <groupId>org.springframework.boot</groupId>
  <artifactId>spring-boot-starter-hateoas</artifactId>
</dependency>
```

One of the important dependencies of `spring-boot-starter-hateoas` is `spring-hateoas`, which provides the HATEOAS features:

```
<dependency>
  <groupId>org.springframework.hateoas</groupId>
  <artifactId>spring-hateoas</artifactId>
</dependency>
```

Let's enhance the `retrieveTodo` resource (/users/{name}/todos/{id}) to return a link to retrieve all `todos` (/users/{name}/todos) in the response:

```
@GetMapping(path = "/users/{name}/todos/{id}")
public Resource<Todo> retrieveTodo(
@PathVariable String name, @PathVariable int id) {
Todo todo = todoService.retrieveTodo(id);
  if (todo == null) {
      throw new TodoNotFoundException("Todo Not Found");
    }

  Resource<Todo> todoResource = new Resource<Todo>(todo);
  ControllerLinkBuilder linkTo =
  linkTo(methodOn(this.getClass()).retrieveTodos(name));
  todoResource.add(linkTo.withRel("parent"));

  return todoResource;
}
```

Some important points to note are as follows:

- `ControllerLinkBuilder linkTo = linkTo(methodOn(this.getClass()).retrieveTodos(name))`: We want to get a link to the `retrieveTodos` method on the current class

- `linkTo.withRel("parent")`: Relationship with the current resource is parent

The following snippet shows the response when a GET request is sent to `http://localhost:8080/users/Jack/todos/1`:

```
{
  "id": 1,
  "user": "Jack",
  "desc": "Learn Spring MVC",
  "targetDate": 1484038262110,
  "done": false,
  "_links": {
          "parent": {
          "href": "http://localhost:8080/users/Jack/todos"
          }
      }
}
```

The `_links` section will contain all the links. Currently, we have one link with the relation parent and `href` as `http://localhost:8080/users/Jack/todos.`:

 If you have problems executing the preceding request, try executing using an Accept header--`application/json`.

HATEOAS is not something that is commonly used in most of the resources today. However, it has the potential to be really useful in reducing the coupling between the service provider and the consumer.

Validation

A good service always validates data before processing it. In this section, we will look at the Bean Validation API and use its reference implementation to implement validation in our services.

The Bean Validation API provides a number of annotations that can be used to validate beans. The **JSR 349** specification defines Bean Validation API 1.1. Hibernate-validator is the reference implementation; both are already defined as dependencies in the `spring-boot-web-starter` project:

- `hibernate-validator-5.2.4.Final.jar`
- `validation-api-1.1.0.Final.jar`

We will create a simple validation for the `createTodo` service method.

Creating validations involves two steps:

1. Enabling validation on the controller method.
2. Adding validations on the bean.

Enabling Validation on the Controller Method

It's very simple to enable validation on the controller method. The following snippet shows an example:

```
@RequestMapping(method = RequestMethod.POST,
path = "/users/{name}/todos")        ResponseEntity<?> add(@
PathVariable String name
    @Valid @RequestBody Todo todo) {
```

The `@Valid(package javax.validation)` annotation is used to mark a parameter for validation. Any validation that is defined in the `Todo` bean is executed before the `add` method is executed.

Defining validations on the Bean

Let's define a few validations on the `Todo` bean:

```
public class Todo {
  private int id;

  @NotNull
  private String user;

  @Size(min = 9, message = "Enter atleast 10 Characters.")
  private String desc;
```

Some important points to note are as follows:

- `@NotNull`: Validates that the user field is not empty
- `@Size(min = 9, message = "Enter atleast 10 Characters.")`: Checks whether the `desc` field has at least nine characters
- There are a number of other annotations that can be used to validate beans. The following are some of the Bean Validation annotations:
- `@AssertFalse, @AssertTrue`: For Boolean elements. Checks the annotated element.
- `@AssertFalse`: Checks for false. `@Assert` checks for true.
- `@Future`: The annotated element must be a date in the future.
- `@Past`: The annotated element must be a date in the past.
- `@Max`: The annotated element must be a number whose value must be lower or equal to the specified maximum.
- `@Min`: The annotated element must be a number whose value must be higher or equal to the specified minimum.
- `@NotNull`: The annotated element cannot be null.
- `@Pattern`: The annotated {@code CharSequence} element must match the specified regular expression. The regular expression follows the Java regular expression conventions.
- `@Size`: The annotated element size must be within the specified boundaries.

Unit Testing Validations

The following example shows how we can unit test the validations we added in:

```
@Test
public void createTodo_withValidationError() throws Exception {
  Todo mockTodo = new Todo(CREATED_TODO_ID, "Jack",
  "Learn Spring MVC", new Date(), false);

  String todo = "{"user":"Jack","desc":"Learn","done":false}";

  when( service.addTodo(
    anyString(), anyString(), isNull(), anyBoolean()))
   .thenReturn(mockTodo);

   MvcResult result = mvc.perform(
   MockMvcRequestBuilders.post("/users/Jack/todos")
   .content(todo)
   .contentType(MediaType.APPLICATION_JSON))
   .andExpect(
      status().is4xxClientError()).andReturn();
}
```

Some important points to note are as follows:

- `"desc":"Learn"`: We are using a `desc` value of length 5. This would cause a validation failure for the `@Size(min = 9, message = "Enter atleast 10 Characters.")` check.

- `.andExpect(status().is4xxClientError())`: Checks for validation error status.

Documenting REST Services

Before a service provider can consume a service, they need a service contract. A service contract defines all the; details about a service:

- How can I call a service? What is the URI of the service?

- What should be the request format?

- What kind of response should I expect?

There are multiple options to define a service contract for RESTful services. The most popular one in the last couple of years is **Swagger**. Swagger is gaining a lot of ground, with support from major vendors in the last couple of years. In this section, we will generate Swagger documentation for our services.

The following quote from the Swagger website (`http://swagger.io`) defines the purpose of the Swagger specification:

Swagger specification creates the RESTful contract for your API, detailing all of its resources and operations in a human and machine readable format for easy development, discovery, and integration.

Generating a Swagger Specification

One of the interesting developments in the last few years of RESTful services development is the evolution of tools to generate service documentation (specification) from the code. This ensures that the code and documentation are always in sync.

Springfox Swagger can be used to generate Swagger documentation from the RESTful services code. What's more, there is a wonderful tool called **Swagger UI**, which, when integrated into the application, provides human-readable documentation.

The following code snippet shows how we can add both these tools; to the; `pom.xml` file:

```
<dependency>
 <groupId>io.springfox</groupId>
 <artifactId>springfox-swagger2</artifactId>
 <version>2.4.0</version>
</dependency>

<dependency>
 <groupId>io.springfox</groupId>
 <artifactId>springfox-swagger-ui</artifactId>
 <version>2.4.0</version>
</dependency>
```

The next step is to add the configuration class to enable and generate Swagger documentation. The following snippet shows how to do it:

```
@Configuration
@EnableSwagger2
public class SwaggerConfig {
  @Bean
  public Docket api() {
    return new Docket(DocumentationType.SWAGGER_2)
    .select()
    .apis(RequestHandlerSelectors.any())
```

```
        .paths(PathSelectors.any()).build();
    }
}
```

Some important points to note are as follows:

- @Configuration: Defines a Spring configuration file
- @EnableSwagger2: The annotation to enable Swagger support
- Docket: A simple builder class to configure the generation of Swagger documentation using the Swagger Spring MVC framework
- new Docket(DocumentationType.SWAGGER_2): Configures Swagger 2 as the Swagger version to be used
- .apis(RequestHandlerSelectors.any()).paths(PathSelectors.any()): Includes all APIs and paths in the documentation

When we bring the server up, we can launch the API Docs URL (http://localhost:8080/v2/api-docs). The following screenshot shows some of the generated documentation:

Let's look at some of the generated documentation. Listed here is the documentation to retrieve the; todos service:

```
"/users/{name}/todos": {
  "get": {
  "tags": [
          "todo-controller"
          ],
  "summary": "retrieveTodos",
  "operationId": "retrieveTodosUsingGET",
  "consumes": [
              "application/json"
              ],
  "produces": [
              "*/*"
              ],
  "parameters": [
          {
            "name": "name",
            "in": "path",
            "description": "name",
            "required": true,
            "type": "string"
          }
          ],
    "responses": {
    "200": {
          "description": "OK",
          "schema": {
                  "type": "array",
                  items": {
                      "$ref": "#/definitions/Todo"
                    }
                  }
          },
    "401": {
          "description": "Unauthorized"
          },
    "403": {
          "description": "Forbidden"
          },
    "404": {
          "description": "Not Found"
          }
      }
    }
  }
```

The service definition clearly defines the request; and response; of the service. Also defined are the different response statuses that the service can return in different situations.

The following code snippet shows the definition of the Todo bean:

```
"Resource«Todo»": {
  "type": "object",
  "properties": {
  "desc": {
          "type": "string"
       },
  "done": {
          "type": "boolean"
       },
  "id": {
          "type": "integer",
          "format": "int32"
      },
  "links": {
          "type": "array",
          "items": {
                 "$ref": "#/definitions/Link"
              }
          },
  "targetDate": {
             "type": "string",
             "format": "date-time"
           },
  "user": {
          "type": "string"
      }
    }
  }
```

It defines all the elements in the Todo bean, along with their formats.

Swagger UI

Swagger UI (`http://localhost:8080/swagger-ui.html`) can also be used to look at the documentation. Swagger UI is enabled by the dependency (`io.springfox:springfox-swagger-ui`) that was added in our `pom.xml`, in the previous step.

Swagger UI (`http://petstore.swagger.io`) is also available online. We can visualize any Swagger documentation (swagger JSON) using Swagger UI.

The following screenshot shows the list of controller-exposing services. When we click on any controller, it expands to show the list of request methods and URIs each controller supports:

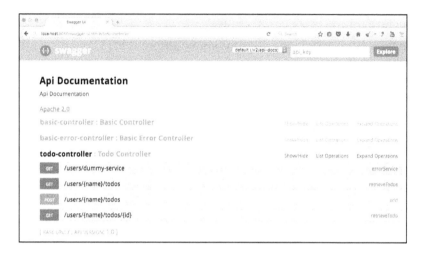

The following screenshot shows the details for the POST service to create a `todo` for the user in Swagger UI:

Some important things to note are as follows:

- `Parameters` show all the important parameters including the request body
- The `Parameter Type` body (for the `todo` parameter) shows the expected structure for the body of the request
- The `Response Messages` sections show different HTTP status codes returned by the service
- The Swagger UI provides an excellent way to expose service definitions for your API without a lot of additional effort.

Customizing Swagger Documentation Using Annotations

The Swagger UI also provides annotations to further customize your documentation.

Listed here is some of the documentation to retrieve the `todos` service:

```
"/users/{name}/todos": {
  "get": {
  "tags": [
          "todo-controller"
          ],
  "summary": "retrieveTodos",
  "operationId": "retrieveTodosUsingGET",
  "consumes": [
          "application/json"
          ],
  "produces": [
          "*/*"
          ],
```

As you can see, the documentation generated is very raw. There are a number of things we can improve in the documentation to describe the services better. Here are a couple of examples:

- Provide a better summary
- Add application/JSON to produces

Swagger provides annotations we can add to our RESTful services in order to customize the documentation. Let's add a few annotations to the controller in order to improve the documentation:

```
@ApiOperation(
    value = "Retrieve all todos for a user by passing in his name",
    notes = "A list of matching todos is returned. Current
pagination
    is not supported.",
    response = Todo.class,
    responseContainer = "List",
    produces = "application/json")
@GetMapping("/users/{name}/todos")
public List<Todo> retrieveTodos(@PathVariable String name) {
    return todoService.retrieveTodos(name);
}
```

A few important points to note are as follows:

- `@ApiOperation(value = "Retrieve all todos for a user by passing in his name")`: Produced in the documentation as a summary of the service

- `notes = "A list of matching todos is returned. Current pagination is not supported."`: Produced in the documentation as a description of the service

- `produces = "application/json"`: Customizes the `produces` section of the service documentation

Here is an extract of the documentation after the update:

```
get": {
    "tags": [
            "todo-controller"
        ],
    "summary": "Retrieve all todos for a user by passing in his
     name",
    "description": "A list of matching todos is returned. Current
     pagination is not supported.",
    "operationId": "retrieveTodosUsingGET",
    "consumes": [
            "application/json"
        ],
    "produces": [
            "application/json",
            "*/*"
        ],
```

Swagger provides a lot of other annotations to customize the documentation. Listed here are some of the important annotations:

- `@Api`: Marks a class as a Swagger resource
- `@ApiModel`: Provides additional information about Swagger models
- `@ApiModelProperty`: Adds and manipulates the data of a model property
- `@ApiOperation`: Describes an operation or an HTTP method against a specific path
- `@ApiParam`: Adds additional metadata for operation parameters
- `@ApiResponse`: Describes an example response of an operation
- `@ApiResponses`: A wrapper to allow a list of multiple `ApiResponse` objects.
- `@Authorization`: Declares an authorization scheme to be used on a resource or an operation
- `@AuthorizationScope`: Describes an OAuth 2 authorization scope
- `@ResponseHeader`: Represents a header that can be provided as part of the response

Swagger provides a few Swagger definition annotations that can be used to customize high-level information about a group of services--contacts, licensing, and other general information. Listed here are some of the important ones:

- `@SwaggerDefinition`: Definition-level properties to be added to the generated Swagger definition
- `@Info`: General metadata for a Swagger definition
- `@Contact`: Properties to describe the person to be contacted for a Swagger definition
- `@License`: Properties to describe the license for a Swagger definition

Securing REST Services with Spring Security

All the services we have created up until now are unsecured. A consumer does not need to provide any credentials to access these services. However, all services in the real world are usually secured.

In this section, we will discuss two ways of authenticating REST services:

- Basic authentication
- OAuth 2.0 authentication

We will implement these two types of authentication with Spring Security.

Spring Boot provides a starter for Spring Security using `spring-boot-starter-security`. We will start with adding Spring Security starter to our `pom.xml` file.

Adding Spring Security Starter

Add the following dependency to your file `pom.xml`:

```
<dependency>
  <groupId>org.springframework.boot</groupId>
  <artifactId>spring-boot-starter-security</artifactId>
</dependency>
```

The `spring-boot-starter-security` dependency brings in three important Spring Security dependencies:

- `spring-security-config`
- `spring-security-core`
- `spring-security-web`

Basic Authentication

The `spring-boot-starter-security` dependency also auto-configures basic authentication for all services by default.

If we try to access any of the services now, we would get `"Access Denied"`.

The response when we send a request to `http://localhost:8080/users/Jack/todos` is shown as an example in the following code snippet:

```
{
  "timestamp": 1484120815039,
  "status": 401,
  "error": "Unauthorized",
  "message": "Full authentication is required to access this
   resource",
   "path": "/users/Jack/todos"
}
```

The response status is `401 - Unauthorized`.

When a resource is secured with basic authentication, we would need to send a user ID and password to authenticate our request. Since we did not configure a user ID and password, Spring Boot auto-configures a default user ID and password. The default user ID is `user`. The default password is usually printed in the log.

An example is shown in the following code snippet:

```
2017-01-11 13:11:58.696 INFO 3888 --- [restartedMain] b.a.s.Authentica
tionManagerConfiguration :

Using default security password: 3fb5564a-ce53-4138-9911-8ade17b2f478

2017-01-11 13:11:58.771 INFO 3888 --- [restartedMain] o.s.s.web.
DefaultSecurityFilterChain : Creating filter chain: Ant [pattern='/
css/**'], []
```

Underlined in the preceding code snippet is the default security password printed in the log.

We can use Postman to fire a request with basic authentication. The following screenshot shows how basic authentication details can be sent along with a request:

As you can see, authentication succeeds and we get a proper response back.

We can configure the user ID and password of our choice in `application.properties`, as shown here:

```
security.user.name=user-name
security.user.password=user-password
```

Spring Security also provides options to authenticate with LDAP or JDBC or any other data source with user credentials.

Integration Testing

The integration test we wrote for the service earlier will start failing because of invalid credentials. We will now update the integration test to supply basic authentication credentials:

```
private TestRestTemplate template = new TestRestTemplate();
HttpHeaders headers = createHeaders("user-name", "user-password");

HttpHeaders createHeaders(String username, String password) {
  return new HttpHeaders() {
    {
      String auth = username + ":" + password;
      byte[] encodedAuth = Base64.getEncoder().encode
      (auth.getBytes(Charset.forName("US-ASCII")));
      String authHeader = "Basic " + new String(encodedAuth);
      set("Authorization", authHeader);
    }
  };
}

@Test
public void retrieveTodos() throws Exception {
  String expected = "["
  + "{id:1,user:Jack,desc:\"Learn Spring MVC\",done:false}" + ","
  + "{id:2,user:Jack,desc:\"Learn Struts\",done:false}" + "]";
  ResponseEntity<String> response = template.exchange(
  createUrl("/users/Jack/todos"), HttpMethod.GET,
  new HttpEntity<String>(null, headers),
  String.class);
  JSONAssert.assertEquals(expected, response.getBody(), false);
}
```

Some important things to note are as follows:

`createHeaders("user-name", "user-password")`: This method creates `Base64.getEncoder().encode` basic authentication headers

`ResponseEntity<String> response = template.exchange(createUrl("/users/Jack/todos"), ;HttpMethod.GET,new HttpEntity<String>(null, headers), String.class)`: The key change is the use of `HttpEntity` to supply the headers that we created earlier to the REST template

Unit Testing

We would not want to use security for our unit tests. The following code snippet shows how we can disable security for the unit test:

```
@RunWith(SpringRunner.class)
@WebMvcTest(value = TodoController.class, secure = false)
public class TodoControllerTest {
```

The key part is the `secure = false` parameter on the `WebMvcTest` annotation. This will disable Spring Security for the unit test.

OAuth 2 Authentication

OAuth is a protocol that provides flows in order to exchange authorization and authentication information between a range of web-enabled applications and services. It enables third-party applications to get restricted access to user information from a service, for example, Facebook, Twitter, or GitHub.

Before we get into the details, it would be useful to review the terminology typically used with respect to OAuth 2 authentication.

Let's consider an example. Let's say we want to expose the `Todo` API to third-party applications on the internet.

The following are the important players in a typical OAuth 2 exchange:

- **Resource owner**: This is the user of the third-party application that wants to use our Todo API. It decides how much of the information available with our API can be made available to the third-party application.
- **Resource server**: This hosts the Todo API, the resource we want to secure.
- **Client**: This is the third-party application that wants to consume our API.
- **Authorization server**: This is the server that provides the OAuth service.

High-level flow

The following steps show a; high-level flow of a typical OAuth authentication:

1. The application requests that the user authorizes access to API resources.

2. When the user provides access, the application receives an authorization grant.

3. The application provides user authorization grant and its own client credentials to the authorization server.

4. If the authentication is successful, the authorization server responds with an access token.

5. The application calls the API (the resource server) that provides the access token for authentication.

6. If the access token is valid, the resource server returns the details of the resource.

Implementing OAuth 2 authentication for Our Service

OAuth 2 for Spring Security (`spring-security-oauth2`) is the module to provide OAuth 2 support to Spring Security. We will add it as a dependency in our `pom.xml` file:

```
<dependency>
  <groupId>org.springframework.security.oauth</groupId>
  <artifactId>spring-security-oauth2</artifactId>
</dependency>
```

Setting up Authorization and Resource Servers:

 The `spring-security-oauth2` has not yet been (June 2017) been updated with the changes for Spring Framework 5.x and Spring Boot 2.x. We will use Spring Boot 1.5.x for examples related to OAuth 2 authentication. Code examples are here in the GitHub repository: `https://github.com/PacktPublishing/Mastering-Spring-5.0`.

Typically, an authorization server would be a different server from the application where the API is exposed. To keep things simple, we will make our current API server act both as the resource server and as the authorization server.

The following code snippet shows how we can enable our application to act as the resource and authorization server:

```
@EnableResourceServer
@EnableAuthorizationServer
@SpringBootApplication
public class Application {
```

Here are a couple of important things to note:

@EnableResourceServer: A convenient annotation for OAuth 2 resource servers, enabling a Spring Security filter that authenticates requests via an incoming OAuth 2 token

@EnableAuthorizationServer: A convenience annotation to enable an authorization server with; AuthorizationEndpoint and; TokenEndpoint in the current application context, which must be a DispatcherServlet context

Now we can configure the access details in application.properties, as shown in the following code snippet:

```
security.user.name=user-name
security.user.password=user-password
security.oauth2.client.clientId: clientId
security.oauth2.client.clientSecret: clientSecret
security.oauth2.client.authorized-grant-types:
authorization_code,refresh_token,password
security.oauth2.client.scope: openid
```

A few important details are as follows:

security.user.name and security.user.password are the authentication details of the resource owner that is an end user of a third-party application

security.oauth2.client.clientId and security.oauth2.client.clientSecret are the authentication details of the client that is the third-party application (the service consumer)

Executing OAuth Requests

We need a two-step process to access the APIs:

1. Obtain an access token.

2. Execute the request using the access token.

Obtaining an Access Token

To get an access token, we call the authorization server (`http://localhost:8080/oauth/token`), providing the client authentication details in the basic authentication mode and the user credentials as part of the form data. The following screenshot shows how we can configure the client authentication details in basic authentication:

The following screenshot shows how to configure the user authentication details as part of the POST parameters:

We are using `grant_type` as the password, indicating that we are sending the user authentication details to get the access token. When we execute the request, we get a response similar to the one shown in the following code snippet:

```
{
    "access_token": "a633dd55-102f-4f53-bcbd-a857df54b821",
    "token_type": "bearer",
    "refresh_token": "d68d89ec-0a13-4224-a29b-e9056768c7f0",
    "expires_in": 43199,
    "scope": "openid"
}
```

Here are a couple of important details:

- `access_token`: Client application can use the access token to authenticate further API calls. However, the access token will expire, typically in a very short time period.
- `refresh_token`: Client application can submit a new request to the authentication server with the `refresh_token` to get a new `access_token`.

Executing the Request Using the Access Token

Once we have `access_token`, we can execute the request using `access_token`, as shown in the following screenshot:

As you can see in the preceding screenshot, we provide the access token in the request header called `Authorization`. We use the value of the format `"Bearer {access_token}"`. Authentication succeeds and we get the expected resource details.

Integration Test

We will now update our integration test to provide the OAuth 2 credentials. The following test highlights the important details:

```
@Test
public void retrieveTodos() throws Exception {
  String expected = "["
```

```
            + "{id:1,user:Jack,desc:\"Learn Spring MVC\",done:false}" + ","
            +"{id:2,user:Jack,desc:\"Learn Struts\",done:false}" + "]";
            String uri = "/users/Jack/todos";
            ResourceOwnerPasswordResourceDetails resource =
            new ResourceOwnerPasswordResourceDetails();
            resource.setUsername("user-name");
            resource.setPassword("user-password");
            resource.setAccessTokenUri(createUrl("/oauth/token"));
            resource.setClientId("clientId");
            resource.setClientSecret("clientSecret");
            resource.setGrantType("password");
            OAuth2RestTemplate oauthTemplate = new
            OAuth2RestTemplate(resource,new
            DefaultOAuth2ClientContext());
            ResponseEntity<String> response =
            oauthTemplate.getForEntity(createUrl(uri), String.class);
          JSONAssert.assertEquals(expected, response.getBody(), false);
        }
```

Some important things to note are as follows:

- `ResourceOwnerPasswordResourceDetails resource = new ResourceOwnerPasswordResourceDetails()`: We set up `ResourceOwnerPasswordResourceDetails` with the user credentials and the client credentials

- `resource.setAccessTokenUri(createUrl("/oauth/token"))`: Configures the URL of the authentication server

- `OAuth2RestTemplate oauthTemplate = new OAuth2RestTemplate(resource,new DefaultOAuth2ClientContext())`: The `OAuth2RestTemplate` is an extension of `RestTemplate`, which supports the OAuth 2 protocol

In this section, we looked at how to enable OAuth 2 authentication in our resources.

Internationalization

Internationalization (i18n) is the process of developing applications and services so that they can be customized for different languages and cultures across the world. It is also called **localization**. The goal of internationalization or localization is to build applications that can offer content in multiple languages and formats.

Spring Boot has built-in support for internationalization.

Let's build a simple service to understand how we can build internationalization in our APIs.

We would need to add a `LocaleResolver` and a message source to our Spring Boot application. The following code snippet should be included in `Application.java`:

```
@Bean
public LocaleResolver localeResolver() {
  SessionLocaleResolver sessionLocaleResolver =
  new SessionLocaleResolver();
  sessionLocaleResolver.setDefaultLocale(Locale.US);
  return sessionLocaleResolver;
}

@Bean
public ResourceBundleMessageSource messageSource() {
  ResourceBundleMessageSource messageSource =
  new ResourceBundleMessageSource();
  messageSource.setBasenames("messages");
  messageSource.setUseCodeAsDefaultMessage(true);
  return messageSource;
}
```

Some important things to note are as follows:

- `sessionLocaleResolver.setDefaultLocale(Locale.US)`: We are a setting a default locale of `Locale.US`.
- `messageSource.setBasenames("messages")`: We're setting the base name of the message source as `messages`. If we are in fr locale (France), we would use messages from `message_fr.properties`. If a message is not available in `message_fr.properties`, it would be searched for in the default `message.properties`.
- `messageSource.setUseCodeAsDefaultMessage(true)`: If a message is not found, then the code is returned as the default message.

Let's configure the messages in the respective files. Let's start with the `messages` properties. The messages in this file would act as the defaults:

```
welcome.message=Welcome in English
```

Let's also configure `messages_fr.properties`. The messages in this file would be used for the locale. If a message is not present here, then the defaults from `messages.properties` will be used:

```
welcome.message=Welcome in French
```

Let's create a service that returns a specific message using the locale specified in the `"Accept-Language"` header:

```
@GetMapping("/welcome-internationalized")
public String msg(@RequestHeader(value = "Accept-Language",
required = false) Locale locale) {
  return messageSource.getMessage("welcome.message", null,
  locale);
}
```

Here are a couple of things to note:

`@RequestHeader(value = "Accept-Language", required = false) Locale locale`: The locale is picked up from the request header `Accept-Language`. It is not required. If a locale is not specified, the default locale is used.

`messageSource.getMessage("welcome.message", null, locale)`: `messageSource` is autowired into the controller. We get the welcome message based on the given locale.

The following screenshot shows the response when the preceding service is called without specifying a default `Accept-Language`:

The default message from `messages.properties` is returned.

The following screenshot shows the response when the preceding service is called with `Accept-Language fr`:

The localized message from `messages_fr.properties` is returned.

In the preceding example, we customized the service to return localized messages based on the locale in the request. A similar approach can be used to internationalize all services in a component.

Caching

Caching data from services plays a crucial role in improving the performance and scalability of applications. In this section, we will look at the implementation options that Spring Boot provides.

Spring provides a caching abstraction based on annotations. We will start with using Spring caching annotations. Later, we will introduce **JSR-107** caching annotations and compare them with Spring abstractions.

Spring-boot-starter-cache

Spring Boot provides a starter project for caching `spring-boot-starter-cache`. Adding this to an application brings in all the dependencies to enable **JSR-107** and Spring caching annotations. The following code snippet shows the dependency details for `spring-boot-starter-cache`. Let's add this to our file `pom.xml`:

```
<dependency>
    <groupId>org.springframework.boot</groupId>
    <artifactId>spring-boot-starter-cache</artifactId>
</dependency>
```

Enabling Caching

Before we can start using caching, we need to enable caching on the application. The following code snippet shows how we can enable caching:

```
@EnableCaching
@SpringBootApplication
public class Application {
```

`@EnableCaching` would enable caching in a Spring Boot application.

Spring Boot automatically configures a suitable CacheManager framework to serve as a provider for the relevant cache. We will look at the details of how Spring Boot decides the CacheManager a little later.

Caching Data

Now that we have enabled caching, we can add the `@Cacheable` annotation to the methods where we want to cache the data. The following code snippet shows how to enable caching on `retrieveTodos`:

```
@Cacheable("todos")
public List<Todo> retrieveTodos(String user) {
```

In the preceding example, the `todos` for a specific user are cached. On the first call to the method for a specific user, the `todos` will be retrieved from the service. On subsequent calls for the same user, the data will be returned from the cache.

Spring also provides conditional caching. In the following snippet, caching is enabled only if the specified condition is satisfied:

```
@Cacheable(cacheNames="todos", condition="#user.length < 10")
public List<Todo> retrieveTodos(String user) {
```

Spring also provides additional annotations to evict data from the cache and add some custom data to cache. A few important ones are listed as follows:

- `@CachePut`: Used to explicitly add data to the cache

- `@CacheEvict`: Used to remove stale data from the cache

- `@Caching`: Allows multiple nested `@Cacheable`, `@CachePut`, and `@CacheEvict` annotations to be used on the same method

JSR-107 Caching Annotations

JSR-107 aims to standardize caching annotations. Listed here are some of the important JSR-107 annotations:

- `@CacheResult`: Similar to `@Cacheable`
- `@CacheRemove`: Similar to `@CacheEvict` `@CacheRemove` supports conditional eviction if an exception occurs
- `@CacheRemoveAll`: Similar to `@CacheEvict(allEntries=true);` used to remove all entries from the cache

JSR-107 and Spring's caching annotations are fairly similar in terms of the features they offer. Either of them is a good choice. We lean slightly toward JSR-107 because it's a standard. However, make sure you are not using both in the same project.

Auto-Detection Order

When caching is enabled, Spring Boot auto-configuration starts looking for a caching provider. The following list shows the order in which Spring Boot searches for caching providers. The list is in order of decreasing preference:

- JCache (JSR-107) (EhCache 3, Hazelcast, Infinispan, and so on)
- EhCache 2.x
- Hazelcast
- Infinispan
- Couchbase
- Redis
- Caffeine
- Guava
- Simple

Summary

Spring Boot makes developing Spring-based applications easy. It enables us to create production-ready applications very quickly.

In this lesson, we covered how to add features such as exception handling, caching, and internationalization to our application. We discussed the best practices of documenting REST services using Swagger. We looked at the basics of securing our microservice with Spring Security.

In the next lesson, we will shift our attention toward advanced features in Spring Boot. We will look at how to provide monitoring on top of our REST services, learn how to deploy the microservice to the Cloud, and understand how to become more productive when developing applications with Spring Boot.

Assessments

1. The _____ provides a number of annotations that can be used to validate beans.

2. Which of the following is an annotated element size that must be within the specified boundaries?

    1. `@SizeOf`

    2. `@SizeBoundary`

    3. `@SizeTo`

    4. `@Size`

3. State whether True or False: HATEOAS is one of the key features of the REST application architecture.

4. Which of the following is a simple builder class to configure the generation of Swagger documentation using the Swagger Spring MVC framework?

    1. Docket

    2. Swagger

    3. REST

    4. QAuth

5. Which of the following is a convenient annotation for OAuth 2 resource servers that enable a Spring Security filter which authenticates requests via an incoming OAuth 2 token?

    1. `@enableResourceServer`

    2. `@enablesResourcesServer`

    3. `@EnableResourceServer`

    4. `@EnableResourceServers`

3
Advanced Spring Boot Features

In the previous lesson, we extended our microservice with exception handling, HATEOAS, caching, and internationalization. In this lesson, let's turn our attention to deploying our services to production. To be able to deploy the services to production, we need to be able to set up and create functionality to configure, deploy, and monitor services.

The following are some of the questions we will answer during this lesson:

- How to externalize application configuration?
- How to use profiles to configure environment-specific values?
- How to deploy our application to the Cloud?
- What is an embedded server? How can you use Tomcat, Jetty, and Undertow?
- What monitoring features does Spring Boot Actuator provide?
- How can you be a more productive developer with Spring Boot?

Externalised Configuration

Applications are typically built once (in JAR or WAR) and then deployed into multiple environments. The following figure shows some of the different environments an application can be deployed to:

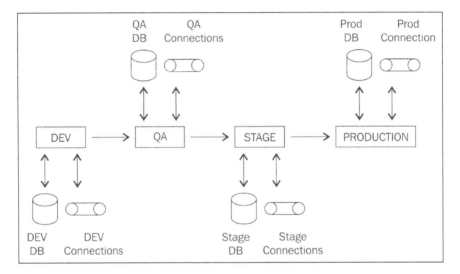

In each of the preceding environments, an application typically has the following:

- Connections to databases
- Connections to multiple services
- Specific environment configurations

It is a good practice to externalize configurations that change between different environments into a configuration file or database.

Spring Boot provides a flexible, standardized approach for externalized configuration.

In this section, we will look at the following:

- How can properties from `application.properties` be used inside our services?
- How do type-safe Configuration Properties make application configuration a cakewalk?
- What kind of support does Spring Boot provide for **Spring Profiles**?
- How can you configure properties in `application.properties`?

In Spring Boot, `application.properties` is the default file from which configuration values are picked up. Spring Boot can pick the `application.properties` file from anywhere on the classpath. Typically, `application.properties` is located at `src\main\resources`, as shown in the following screenshot:

In *Lesson 2*, *Extending Microservices*, we looked at examples of customizing Spring Security using configuration in `application.properties`:

```
security.basic.enabled=false
management.security.enabled=false
security.user.name=user-name
security.user.password=user-password
security.oauth2.client.clientId: clientId
security.oauth2.client.clientSecret: clientSecret
security.oauth2.client.authorized-grant-types:
authorization_code,refresh_token,password
security.oauth2.client.scope: openid
```

Similar to these, all other Spring Boot starters, modules, and frameworks can be customized through configuration in `application.properties`. In the next section, let's look at some of the configuration options Spring Boot provides for these frameworks.

Customizing Frameworks Through application.properties

In this section, we will discuss some of the important things that can be configured through `application.properties`.

 For the complete list, refer to `https://docs.spring.io/spring-boot/docs/current-SNAPSHOT/reference/htmlsingle/#common-application-properties`.

Logging

Some of the things that can be configured are as follows:

- The location of the logging configuration file
- the location of the log file
- Logging level

The following snippet shows a few examples:

```
# Location of the logging configuration file.
  logging.config=
# Log file name.
  logging.file=
# Configure Logging level.
# Example `logging.level.org.springframework=TRACE`
  logging.level.*=
```

Embedded Server Configuration

An embedded server is one of the most important features of Spring Boot. Some of the embedded server features that can be configured through application properties include:

- Server ports
- SSL support and configuration
- Access log configuration

The following snippet shows some of the embedded server features that can be configured through application properties:

```
# Path of the error controller.
server.error.path=/error
# Server HTTP port
server.port=8080
# Enable SSL support.
server.ssl.enabled=
# Path to key store with SSL certificate
server.ssl.key-store=
# Key Store Password
server.ssl.key-store-password=
# Key Store Provider
server.ssl.key-store-provider=
# Key Store Type
```

```
server.ssl.key-store-type=
# Should we enable access log of Tomcat?
server.tomcat.accesslog.enabled=false
# Maximum number of connections that server can accept
server.tomcat.max-connections=
```

Spring MVC

Spring MVC can be extensively configured through `application.properties`. Listed here are some of the important configurations:

```
# Date format to use. For instance `dd/MM/yyyy`.
 spring.mvc.date-format=
# Locale to use.
 spring.mvc.locale=
# Define how the locale should be resolved.
 spring.mvc.locale-resolver=accept-header
# Should "NoHandlerFoundException" be thrown if no Handler is found?
 spring.mvc.throw-exception-if-no-handler-found=false
# Spring MVC view prefix. Used by view resolver.
 spring.mvc.view.prefix=
# Spring MVC view suffix. Used by view resolver.
 spring.mvc.view.suffix=
```

Spring Starter Security

Spring Security can be extensively configured through `application.properties`. The following examples show some of the important configuration options related to Spring Security:

```
# Set true to Enable basic authentication
 security.basic.enabled=true
# Provide a Comma-separated list of uris you would want to secure
 security.basic.path=/**
# Provide a Comma-separated list of paths you don't want to secure
 security.ignored=
# Name of the default user configured by spring security
 security.user.name=user
# Password of the default user configured by spring security.
 security.user.password=
# Roles granted to default user
 security.user.role=USER
```

Data Sources, JDBC, and JPA

Data Sources, JDBC, and JPA can also be extensively configured through
`application.properties`. Listed here are some of the important options:

```
# Fully qualified name of the JDBC driver.
 spring.datasource.driver-class-name=
# Populate the database using 'data.sql'.
 spring.datasource.initialize=true
# JNDI location of the datasource.
 spring.datasource.jndi-name=
# Name of the datasource.
 spring.datasource.name=testdb
# Login password of the database.
 spring.datasource.password=
# Schema (DDL) script resource references.
 spring.datasource.schema=
# Db User to use to execute DDL scripts
 spring.datasource.schema-username=
# Db password to execute DDL scripts
 spring.datasource.schema-password=
# JDBC url of the database.
 spring.datasource.url=
# JPA - Initialize the schema on startup.
 spring.jpa.generate-ddl=false
# Use Hibernate's newer IdentifierGenerator for AUTO, TABLE and
SEQUENCE.
 spring.jpa.hibernate.use-new-id-generator-mappings=
# Enable logging of SQL statements.
 spring.jpa.show-sql=false
```

Other Configuration Options

Some other things that can be configured through `application.properties` are
as follows:

* Profiles
* HTTP message converters (Jackson/JSON)
* Transaction management
* Internationalization

The following examples show some of the configuration options:

```
# Comma-separated list (or list if using YAML) of active profiles.
 spring.profiles.active=
# HTTP message conversion. jackson or gson
 spring.http.converters.preferred-json-mapper=jackson
# JACKSON Date format string. Example `yyyy-MM-dd HH:mm:ss`.
 spring.jackson.date-format=
# Default transaction timeout in seconds.
 spring.transaction.default-timeout=
# Perform the rollback on commit failures.
 spring.transaction.rollback-on-commit-failure=
# Internationalization : Comma-separated list of basenames
 spring.messages.basename=messages
# Cache expiration for resource bundles, in sec. -1 will cache for
ever
 spring.messages.cache-seconds=-1
```

Custom Properties in Application.Properties

Until now, we have looked at using prebuilt properties provided by Spring Boot for various frameworks. In this section, we will look at creating our application-specific configuration that can also be configured in `application.properties`.

Let's consider an example. We want to be able to interact with an external service. We want to be able to externalize the configuration of the URL of this service.

The following example shows how we would want to configure the external service in `application.properties`:

```
somedataservice.url=http://abc.service.com/something
```

We want to use the value of the `somedataservice.url` property in our data service. The following snippet shows how we can do that in an example data service.

```
@Component
public class SomeDataService {
  @Value("${somedataservice.url}")
  private String url;
  public String retrieveSomeData() {
    // Logic using the url and getting the data
   return "data from service";
  }
}
```

A couple of important things to note are as follows:

- `@Component public class SomeDataService`: The data service bean is managed by Spring because of the `@Component` annotation.
- `@Value("${somedataservice.url}")`: The value of `somedataservice.url` will be autowired into the `url` variable. The `url` value can be used in the methods of the bean.

Configuration properties - Type-Safe Configuration Management

While the `@Value` annotation provides dynamic configuration, it also has several drawbacks:

- If we want to use three property values in a service, we would need to autowire them using `@Value` three times.
- The `@Value` annotations and the keys of the messages would be spread across the application. If we want to find the list of the configurable values in an application, we have to search through the application for `@Value` annotations.

Spring Boot provides a better approach to application configuration through the strongly typed `ConfigurationProperties` feature. This allows us to do the following:

- Have all the properties in a predefined bean structure
- This bean would act as the centralized store for all application properties
- The configuration bean can be autowired wherever application configuration is needed

An example configuration bean is shown as follows:

```
@Component
@ConfigurationProperties("application")
public class ApplicationConfiguration {
  private boolean enableSwitchForService1;
  private String service1Url;
  private int service1Timeout;
  public boolean isEnableSwitchForService1() {
    return enableSwitchForService1;
  }
  public void setEnableSwitchForService1
  (boolean enableSwitchForService1) {
    this.enableSwitchForService1 = enableSwitchForService1;
```

```
    }
    public String getService1Url() {
      return service1Url;
    }
    public void setService1Url(String service1Url) {
      this.service1Url = service1Url;
    }
    public int getService1Timeout() {
      return service1Timeout;
    }
    public void setService1Timeout(int service1Timeout) {
      this.service1Timeout = service1Timeout;
    }
  }
}
```

A couple of important things to note are as follows:

- `@ConfigurationProperties("application")` is the annotation for an externalized configuration. We can add this annotation to any class to bind to external properties. The value in the double quotes--application--is used as a prefix while binding external configuration to this bean.
- We are defining multiple configurable values in the bean.
- Getters and setters are needed since binding happens through Java beans property descriptors.

The following snippet shows how the values for these properties can be defined in `application.properties`:

```
application.enableSwitchForService1=true
application.service1Url=http://abc-dev.service.com/somethingelse
application.service1Timeout=250
```

A couple of important things to note are as follows:

- `application`: The prefix is defined as part of `@ConfigurationProperties("application")` while defining the configuration bean
- Values are defined by appending the prefix to the name of the property

We can use configuration properties in other beans by autowiring `ApplicationConfiguration` into the bean:

```
@Component
public class SomeOtherDataService {
  @Autowired
  private ApplicationConfiguration configuration;
```

```
public String retrieveSomeData() {
    // Logic using the url and getting the data
    System.out.println(configuration.getService1Timeout());
    System.out.println(configuration.getService1Url());
    System.out.println(configuration.isEnableSwitchForService1());
    return "data from service";
  }
}
```

A couple of important things to note are as follows:

- `@Autowired private ApplicationConfiguration configuration`: `ApplicationConfiguration` is autowired into `SomeOtherDataService`
- `configuration.getService1Timeout()`, `configuration.getService1Url()`, `configuration.isEnableSwitchForService1()`: Values can be accessed in bean methods using the getter methods on the configuration bean

By default, any failure in binding externally configured values to configuration properties bean would result in the failure of the server start up. This prevents problems that arise because of misconfigured applications running in production.

Let's use the misconfigure service timeout to see what happens:

```
application.service1Timeout=SOME_MISCONFIGURATION
```

The application will fail to start up with an error.

```
***************************
 APPLICATION FAILED TO START
***************************
Description:
Binding to target com.mastering.spring.springboot.configuration.Applic
ationConfiguration@79d3473e failed:

Property: application.service1Timeout
Value: SOME_MISCONFIGURATION
Reason: Failed to convert property value of type 'java.lang.String' to
required type 'int' for property 'service1Timeout'; nested exception
is org.springframework.core.convert.ConverterNotFoundException: No
converter found capable of converting from type [java.lang.String] to
type [int]

Action:
Update your application's configuration
```

Profiles

Until now, we looked at how to externalize application configuration to a property file, `application.properties`. What we want to be able to do is have different values for the same property in different environments.

Profiles provide a way to provide different configurations in different environments.

The following snippet shows how to configure an active profile in `application.properties`:

```
spring.profiles.active=dev
```

Once you have an active profile configured, you can define properties specific to that profile in `application-{profile-name}.properties`. For `dev` profile, the name of the properties file would be `application-dev.properties`. The following example shows the configuration in `application-dev.properties`:

```
application.enableSwitchForService1=true
application.service1Url=http://abc-dev.service.com/somethingelse
application.service1Timeout=250
```

The values in `application-dev.properties` will override the default configuration in `application.properties`if the active profile is `dev`.

We can have configurations for multiple environments, as shown here:

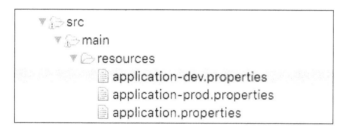

Profiles-Based Bean Configuration

Profiles can also be used to define different beans or different bean configurations in different environments. All classes marked with `@Component` or `@Configuration` can also be marked with an additional `@Profile` annotation to specify the profile in which the bean or configuration is enabled.

Let's consider an example. An application needs different caches enabled in different environments. In the `dev` environment, it uses a very simple cache. In production, we would want to use a distributed cache. This can be implemented using profiles.

The following bean shows the configuration enabled in a `dev` environment:

```
@Profile("dev")
@Configuration
public class DevSpecificConfiguration {
  @Bean
  public String cache() {
    return "Dev Cache Configuration";
  }
}
```

The following bean shows the configuration enabled in a production environment:

```
@Profile("prod")
@Configuration
public class ProdSpecificConfiguration {
  @Bean
  public String cache() {
    return "Production Cache Configuration - Distributed Cache";
  }
}
```

Based on the active profile configured, the respective configuration is picked up. Note that we are not really configuring a distributed cache in this example. We are returning a simple string to illustrate that profiles can be used to implement these kinds of variations.

Other Options for Application Configuration Values

Until now, the approaches we took to configure application properties was using the key value pairs from either `application.properties` or `application-{profile-name}.properties`.

Spring Boot provides a number of other ways to configure application properties.

Listed here are some of the important ways of providing application configuration:

- Command-line arguments
- Creating a system property with the name SPRING_APPLICATION_JSON and including the JSON configuration
- `ServletConfig` init parameters
- `ServletContext` init parameters

- Java System properties (`System.getProperties()`)

- Operating system environment variables

- Profile-specific application properties outside of `.jar`, somewhere in the classpath of the application (`application-{profile}.properties`)

- Profile-specific application properties packaged inside your `.jar` (`application-{profile}.properties` and YAML variants)

- Application properties outside the `.jar`

- Application properties packaged inside the `.jar`

More information can be found in the Spring Boot documentation at: `http://docs.spring.io/spring-boot/docs/current-SNAPSHOT/reference/htmlsingle/#boot-features-external-config`.

The approaches at the top of this list have higher priority than those at the bottom of the list. For example, if a command-line argument with the name `spring.profiles.active` is provided when launching the application, it would override any configuration provided through `application.properties` because command-line arguments have higher preference.

This provides great flexibility in determining how you would want to configure your application in different environments.

YAML Configuration

Spring Boot also supports YAML to configure your properties.

YAML is an abbreviation for **YAML Ain't Markup Language**. It is a human readable structured format. YAML is commonly used for configuration files.

To understand basic syntax of YAML, look at the example below (`application.yaml`). This shows how our application configuration can be specified in YAML.

```
spring:
  profiles:
    active: prod
security:
  basic:
    enabled: false
  user:
    name=user-name
    password=user-password
oauth2:
```

```
        client:
            clientId: clientId
            clientSecret: clientSecret
            authorized-grant-types: authorization_code,refresh_
token,password
            scope: openid
        application:
            enableSwitchForService1: true
            service1Url: http://abc-dev.service.com/somethingelse
            service1Timeout: 250
```

As you can see, the YAML configuration is much more readable than `application.properties`, as it allows better grouping of properties.

Another advantage of YAML is that it allows you to specify the configuration for multiple profiles in a single configuration file. The following snippet shows an example:

```
application:
  service1Url: http://service.default.com
---
spring:
  profiles: dev
  application:
    service1Url: http://service.dev.com
---
spring:
  profiles: prod
  application:
    service1Url: http://service.prod.com
```

In this example, `http://service.dev.com` will be used in the `dev` profile, and `http://service.prod.com` is used in the `prod` profile. In all other profiles, `http://service.default.com` will be used as the service URL.

Embedded Servers

One of the important concepts Spring Boot brings in is embedded servers.

Let's first understand the difference between traditional Java web application deployment and this new concept called embedded server.

Traditionally, with Java web applications, we build **Web Application Archive (WAR)** or **Enterprise Application Archive (EAR)** and deploy them into servers. Before we can deploy a WAR on the server, we need a web server or an application server installed on the server. The application server would be on top of the Java instance installed on the server. So, we need Java and an application (or web server) installed on the machine before we can deploy our application. The following figure shows an example installation in Linux:

Spring Boot brings in the concept of embedded servers, where the web server is part of the application deployable--JAR. To deploy applications using embedded servers, it is sufficient if Java is installed on the server. The following figure shows an example installation:

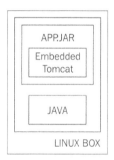

When we build any application with Spring Boot, the default is to build a JAR. With `spring-boot-starter-web`, the default embedded server is Tomcat.

When we use `spring-boot-starter-web`, a few Tomcat-related dependencies can be seen in the Maven dependencies section. These dependencies will be included as part of the application deployment package:

```
▶ tomcat-embed-core-8.5.6.jar - /Users
▶ tomcat-embed-el-8.5.6.jar - /Users/ra
▶ tomcat-embed-websocket-8.5.6.jar - /
```

To deploy the application, we need to build a JAR. We can build a JAR using the command below:

```
mvn clean install
```

The following screenshot shows the structure of the JAR created.

`BOOT-INF\classes` contains all application-related class files (from `src\main\java`) as well as the application properties from `src\main\resources`:

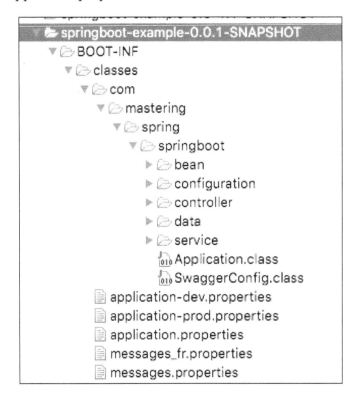

Some of the libraries in `BOOT-INF\lib` are shown in the following screenshot:

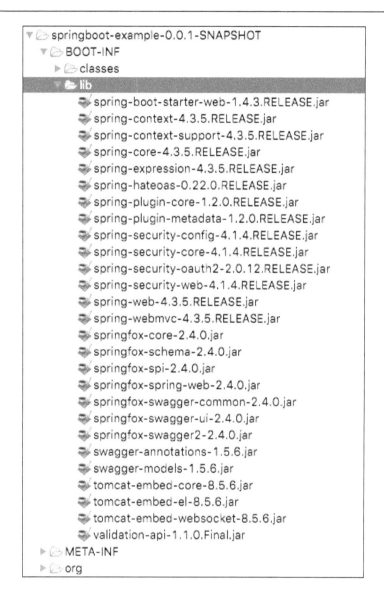

BOOT-INF\lib contains all the JAR dependencies of the application. There are three Tomcat-specific JARs among these. These three JARs enable the launch of an embedded Tomcat service when the application is run as a Java application. Because of this, a Java installation is sufficient to deploy this application on a server.

Switching to Jetty and Undertow

The following screenshot shows the changes needed in order to switch to using Jetty embedded server:

```
<dependency>
    <groupId>org.springframework.boot</groupId>
    <artifactId>spring-boot-starter-web</artifactId>
    <exclusions>
        <exclusion>
            <groupId>org.springframework.boot</groupId>
            <artifactId>spring-boot-starter-tomcat</artifactId>
        </exclusion>
    </exclusions>
</dependency>

<dependency>
    <groupId>org.springframework.boot</groupId>
    <artifactId>spring-boot-starter-jetty</artifactId>
</dependency>
```

All that we need to do is exclude the Tomcat starter dependency in `spring-boot-starter-web` and include a dependency in `spring-boot-starter-jetty`.

You can now see a number of Jetty dependencies in the Maven dependencies section. The following screenshot shows a few of the Jetty-related dependencies:

```
▶ jetty-servlets-9.3.14.v20161028.jar - /Us
▶ jetty-continuation-9.3.14.v20161028.jar
▶ jetty-http-9.3.14.v20161028.jar - /Users/
▶ jetty-util-9.3.14.v20161028.jar - /Users/r
▶ jetty-io-9.3.14.v20161028.jar - /Users/ra
▶ jetty-webapp-9.3.14.v20161028.jar - /Us
▶ jetty-xml-9.3.14.v20161028.jar - /Users/
▶ jetty-servlet-9.3.14.v20161028.jar - /Use
▶ jetty-security-9.3.14.v20161028.jar - /Us
▶ jetty-server-9.3.14.v20161028.jar - /Use
```

Switching to Undertow is equally easy. Use `spring-boot-starter-undertow` instead of `spring-boot-starter-jetty`:

```
<dependency>
  <groupId>org.springframework.boot</groupId>
  <artifactId>spring-boot-starter-undertow</artifactId>
</dependency>
```

Building a WAR file

Spring Boot also provides the option of building a traditional WAR file instead of using a JAR.

First, we need to change our packaging in `pom.xml` to `WAR`:

```
<packaging>war</packaging>
```

We would want to prevent tomcat server to be embedded as a dependency in the WAR file. We can do this by modifying the dependency on the embedded server (Tomcat in the following example) to have a scope of provided. The following snippet shows the exact details:

```
<dependency>
  <groupId>org.springframework.boot</groupId>
  <artifactId>spring-boot-starter-tomcat</artifactId>
  <scope>provided</scope>
</dependency>
```

When you build the WAR file, Tomcat dependencies are not included. We can use this WAR to deploy on an application server, such as WebSphere or Weblogic, or a web server, such as Tomcat.

Developer Tools

Spring Boot provides tools that can improve the experience of developing Spring Boot applications. One of these is Spring Boot developer tools.

To use Spring Boot developer tools, we need to include a dependency:

```
<dependencies>
 <dependency>
   <groupId>org.springframework.boot</groupId>
   <artifactId>spring-boot-devtools</artifactId>
   <optional>true</optional>
 </dependency>
</dependencies>
```

Spring Boot developer tools, by default, disables the caching of view templates and static files. This enables a developer to see the changes as soon as they make them.

Another important feature is the automatic restart when any file in the classpath changes. So, the application automatically restarts in the following scenarios:

- When we make a change to a controller or a service class
- When we make a change to the property file

The advantages of Spring Boot developer tools are as follows:

- The developer does not need to stop and start the application each time. The application is automatically restarted as soon as there is a change.
- The restart feature in Spring Boot developer tools is intelligent. It only reloads the actively developed classes. It does not reload the third-party JARs (using two different class-loaders). Thereby, the restart when something in the application changes is much faster compared to cold-starting an application.

Live Reload

Another useful Spring Boot developer tools feature is **live reload**. You can download a specific plugin for your browser from `http://livereload.com/extensions/`.

You can enable live reload by clicking on the button in the browser. The button in the Safari browser is shown in the following screenshot. It's in the top-left corner beside the address bar.

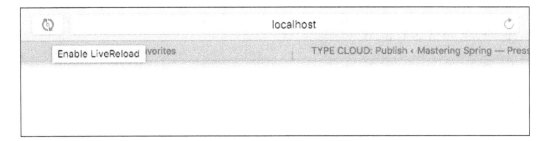

If there are code changes made on the pages or services that are shown in the browser, they are auto-refreshed with new content. There is no need to hit that refresh button anymore!

Spring Boot Actuator

When an application is deployed into production:

- We want to know immediately if some service goes down or is very slow

- We want to know immediately if any of the servers does not have sufficient free space or memory

This is called **application monitoring**.

Spring Boot Actuator provides a number of production-ready monitoring features.

We will add Spring Boot Actuator by adding a simple dependency:

```
<dependencies>
  <dependency>
    <groupId>org.springframework.boot</groupId>
    <artifactId>spring-boot-starter-actuator</artifactId>
  </dependency>
</dependencies>
```

As soon as the actuator is added to an application, it enables a number of endpoints. When we start the application, we see a number of added new mappings. The following screenshot shows an extract of these new mappings from the start up log:

The actuator exposes a number of endpoints. The actuator endpoint (`http://localhost:8080/application`) acts as a discovery for all other endpoints. The following screenshot shows the response when we execute the request from a Postman:

HAL Browser

A number of these endpoints expose a lot of data. To be able to visualize the information better, we will add an **HAL Browser** to our application:

```
<dependency>
    <groupId>org.springframework.data</groupId>
    <artifactId>spring-data-rest-hal-browser</artifactId>
</dependency>
```

Spring Boot Actuator exposes REST APIs around all the data captured from the Spring Boot application and environment. The HAL Browser enables visual representation around the Spring Boot Actuator API:

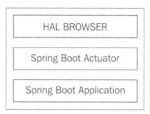

When we launch `http://localhost:8080/application` in the browser, we can see all the URLs exposed by actuator.

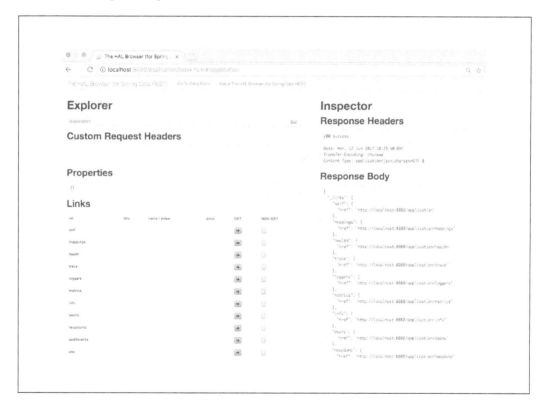

Let's browse all the information exposed by actuator as part of different endpoints through the HAL Browser.

Configuration Properties

The `configprops` endpoint provides information about configuration options that can be configured through application properties. It basically is a collated list of all `@ConfigurationProperties`. The following screenshot shows `configprops` in HAL Browser:

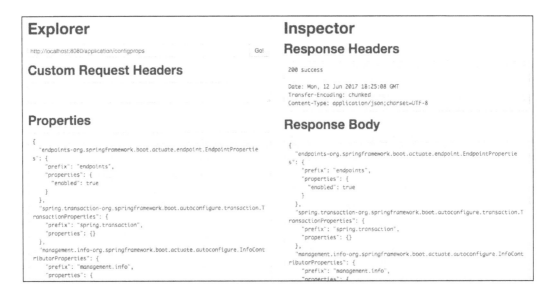

To illustrate a known example, the following section from the service response shows the configuration options available for Spring MVC:

```
"spring.mvc-  org.springframework.boot.autoconfigure.web.
WebMvcProperties": {
    "prefix": "spring.mvc",
    "properties": {
                    "dateFormat": null,
                    "servlet": {
                      "loadOnStartup": -1
                    },
    "staticPathPattern": "/**",
    "dispatchOptionsRequest": true,
    "dispatchTraceRequest": false,
    "locale": null,
    "ignoreDefaultModelOnRedirect": true,
    "logResolvedException": true,
    "async": {
                    "requestTimeout": null
                },
    "messageCodesResolverFormat": null,
```

```
      "mediaTypes": {},
      "view": {
              "prefix": null,
              "suffix": null
          },
      "localeResolver": "ACCEPT_HEADER",
      "throwExceptionIfNoHandlerFound": false
        }
}
```

 To provide configuration for Spring MVC, we combine the prefix with the path in properties. For example, to configure `loadOnStartup`, we use a property with the name `spring.mvc.servlet.loadOnStartup`.

Environment Details

The **environment (env)** endpoint provides information about the operating system, JVM installation, classpath, system environment variable, and the values configured in various application properties files. The following screenshot shows the environment endpoint in the HAL Browser:

Explorer

http://localhost:8080/application/env   Go!

Custom Request Headers

Properties

```
{
  "profiles": [
    "dev"
  ],
  "server.ports": {
    "local.server.port": 8080
  },
  "servletContextInitParams": {},
  "systemProperties": {
    "java.runtime.name": "Java(TM) SE Runtime Environment",
    "sun.boot.library.path": "/Library/Java/JavaVirtualMachines/jdk1.8.0_31.jdk/Contents/Home/jre/lib",
    "java.vm.version": "25.31-b07",
    "user.country.format": "IN",
    "gopherProxySet": "false",
    "java.vm.vendor": "Oracle Corporation",
    "java.vendor.url": "http://java.oracle.com/",
    "path.separator": ":",
    "java.vm.name": "Java HotSpot(TM) 64-Bit Server VM",
    "file.encoding.pkg": "sun.io",
    "user.country": "US",
```

Inspector

Response Headers

200 success

Date: Mon, 12 Jun 2017 18:25:48 GMT
Transfer-Encoding: chunked
Content-Type: application/json;charset=UTF-8

Response Body

```
{
  "profiles": [
    "dev"
  ],
  "server.ports": {
    "local.server.port": 8080
  },
  "servletContextInitParams": {},
  "systemProperties": {
    "java.runtime.name": "Java(TM) SE Runtime Environment",
    "sun.boot.library.path": "/Library/Java/JavaVirtualMachines/jdk1.8.0_31.jdk/Contents/Home/jre/lib",
    "java.vm.version": "25.31-b07",
    "user.country.format": "IN",
    "gopherProxySet": "false",
    "java.vm.vendor": "Oracle Corporation",
    "java.vendor.url": "http://java.oracle.com/",
    "path.separator": ":",
    "java.vm.name": "Java HotSpot(TM) 64-Bit Server VM",
    "file.encoding.pkg": "sun.io",
```

An extract from the response from the /application/env service is shown here. It shows a few system details as well as the details from application configuration:

```
"systemEnvironment": {
    "JAVA_MAIN_CLASS_13377": "com.mastering.spring.springboot.
Application",
    "PATH": "/usr/bin:/bin:/usr/sbin:/sbin",
    "SHELL": "/bin/bash",
    "JAVA_STARTED_ON_FIRST_THREAD_13019": "1",
    "APP_ICON_13041": "../Resources/Eclipse.icns",
    "USER": "rangaraokaranam",
    "TMPDIR": "/var/folders/y_/x4jdvdkx7w94q5qsh745gzz00000gn/T/",
    "SSH_AUTH_SOCK": "/private/tmp/com.apple.launchd.IcESePQCLV/
Listeners",
    "XPC_FLAGS": "0x0",
    "JAVA_STARTED_ON_FIRST_THREAD_13041": "1",
    "APP_ICON_11624": "../Resources/Eclipse.icns",
    "LOGNAME": "rangaraokaranam",
    "XPC_SERVICE_NAME": "0",
    "HOME": "/Users/rangaraokaranam"
},
"applicationConfig: [classpath:/application-prod.properties]": {
    "application.service1Timeout": "250",
    "application.service1Url": "http://abc-    prod.service.com/
somethingelse",
    "application.enableSwitchForService1": "false"
},
```

Health

The health service provides details of the disk space and status of the application. The following screenshot shows the service executed from the HAL Browser:

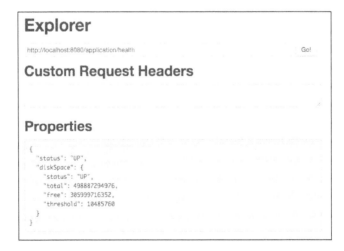

Mappings

The mappings endpoint provides information about different service endpoints that are exposed from the application:

- URI

- Request methods

- Bean

- Controller methods exposing the service

Mappings provides a collated list of all `@RequestMapping` paths. An extract from the response of the `/application/mappings` endpoint is shown here:

```
"{[/welcome-internationalized],methods=[GET]}": {
   "bean": "requestMappingHandlerMapping",
   "method": "public java.lang.String
    com.mastering.spring.springboot.controller.
    BasicController.msg(java.uti l.Locale)"
},
"{[/welcome],methods=[GET]}": {
   "bean": "requestMappingHandlerMapping",
   "method": "public java.lang.String
    com.mastering.spring.springboot.controller.
    BasicController.welcome()"
},
"{[/welcome-with-object],methods=[GET]}": {
    "bean": "requestMappingHandlerMapping",
    "method": "public com.mastering.spring.springboot.
     bean.WelcomeBeancom.mastering.spring.springboot.
     controller.BasicController.welcomeWithObject()"
},
"{[/welcome-with-parameter/name/{name}],methods=[GET]}": {
    "bean": "requestMappingHandlerMapping",
    "method": "public
     com.mastering.spring.springboot.bean.WelcomeBean
     com.mastering.spring.springboot.controller.
     BasicController.welcomeWithParameter(java.lang.String)"
},
"{[/users/{name}/todos],methods=[POST]}": {
    "bean": "requestMappingHandlerMapping",
    "method": "org.springframework.http.ResponseEntity<?>
     com.mastering.spring.springboot.controller.
     TodoController.add(java.lang.String,com.mastering.spring.
     springboot.bean.Todo)"
```

```
    },
"{[/users/{name}/todos],methods=[GET]}": {
        "bean": "requestMappingHandlerMapping",
        "method": "public java.util.List<com.mastering.spring.
         springboot.bean.Todo>
         com.mastering.spring.springboot.controller.
         TodoController.retrieveTodos(java.lang.String)"
    },
"{[/users/{name}/todos/{id}],methods=[GET]}": {
        "bean": "requestMappingHandlerMapping",
        "method": "public
         org.springframework.hateoas.Resource<com.mastering.
         spring.springboot.bean.Todo>
         com.mastering.spring.springboot.controller.
         TodoController.retrieveTodo(java.lang.String,int)"
    },
```

Beans

The beans endpoint provides the details about the beans that are loaded into the Spring context. This is useful in debugging any problems related to Spring context.

```
An extract from the response of the /application/beans endpoint is
shown below:    {
    "bean": "basicController",
    "aliases": [],
    "scope": "singleton",
    "type": "com.mastering.spring.springboot.
     controller.BasicController",
    "resource": "file [/in28Minutes/Workspaces/
     SpringTutorial/mastering-spring-lesson-5-6-
     7/target/classes/com/mastering/spring/springboot/
     controller/BasicController.class]",
    "dependencies": [
                    "messageSource"
                ]
},
{
    "bean": "todoController",
    "aliases": [],
    "scope": "singleton",
    "type": "com.mastering.spring.springboot.
     controller.TodoController",
    "resource": "file [/in28Minutes/Workspaces/SpringTutorial/
```

```
mastering-spring-lesson-5-6-
7/target/classes/com/mastering/spring/
springboot/controller/TodoController.class]",
        "dependencies": [
                "todoService"
                ]
}
```

It shows the details for two beans: basicController and todoController. You can see the following details for all the beans:

- The name of the bean and its aliases
- The scope of the bean
- The type of the bean
- The exact location of the class from which this bean is created
- Dependencies of the bean

Metrics

The metrics endpoint shows some of the important metrics about the following:

- Server--free memory, processors, uptime, and so on
- JVM--details about the heap, threads, garbage collection, sessions, and so on
- Responses provided by application services

An extract from the response of the /application/metrics endpoint is shown as follows:

```
{
"mem": 481449,
"mem.free": 178878,
"processors": 4,
"instance.uptime": 1853761,
"uptime": 1863728,
"systemload.average": 2.3349609375,
"heap.committed": 413696,
"heap.init": 65536,
"heap.used": 234817,
"heap": 932352,
"nonheap.committed": 69248,
"nonheap.init": 2496,
"nonheap.used": 67754,
"nonheap": 0,
```

```
"threads.peak": 23,
"threads.daemon": 21,
"threads.totalStarted": 30,
"threads": 23,
"classes": 8077,
"classes.loaded": 8078,
"classes.unloaded": 1,
"gc.ps_scavenge.count": 15,
"gc.ps_scavenge.time": 242,
"gc.ps_marksweep.count": 3,
"gc.ps_marksweep.time": 543,
"httpsessions.max": -1,
"httpsessions.active": 0,
"gauge.response.actuator": 8,
"gauge.response.mappings": 12,
"gauge.response.beans": 83,
"gauge.response.health": 14,
"gauge.response.root": 9,
"gauge.response.heapdump": 4694,
"gauge.response.env": 6,
"gauge.response.profile": 12,
"gauge.response.browser.star-star": 10,
"gauge.response.actuator.root": 2,
"gauge.response.configprops": 272,
"gauge.response.actuator.star-star": 13,
"counter.status.200.profile": 1,
"counter.status.200.actuator": 8,
"counter.status.200.mappings": 1,
"counter.status.200.root": 5,
"counter.status.200.configprops": 1,
"counter.status.404.actuator.star-star": 3,
"counter.status.200.heapdump": 1,
"counter.status.200.health": 1,
"counter.status.304.browser.star-star": 132,
"counter.status.302.actuator.root": 4,
"counter.status.200.browser.star-star": 37,
"counter.status.200.env": 2,
"counter.status.302.root": 5,
"counter.status.200.beans": 1,
"counter.status.200.actuator.star-star": 210,
"counter.status.302.actuator": 1
}
```

Auto-Configuration

Auto-configuration is one of the most important features of Spring Boot. The auto-configuration endpoint (/application/autoconfig) exposes the details related to auto-configuration. It shows both positive matches and negative matches with details about why a particular auto-configuration succeeded or failed.

The following extract shows some of the positive matches from the response:

```
"positiveMatches": {
  "AuditAutoConfiguration#auditListener": [
    {
      "condition": "OnBeanCondition",
      "message": "@ConditionalOnMissingBean (types:
      org.springframework.boot.actuate.audit.
      listener.AbstractAuditListener; SearchStrategy: all) did not
find
      any beans"
    }
  ],
  "AuditAutoConfiguration#authenticationAuditListener": [
  {
    "condition": "OnClassCondition",
    "message": "@ConditionalOnClass found required class
    'org.springframework.security.authentication.
    event.AbstractAuthenticationEvent'"
  },
```

The following extract shows some of the negative matches from the response:

```
"negativeMatches": {
  "CacheStatisticsAutoConfiguration.
  CaffeineCacheStatisticsProviderConfiguration": [
  {
    "condition": "OnClassCondition",
    "message": "@ConditionalOnClass did not find required class
    'com.github.benmanes.caffeine.cache.Caffeine'"
  }
  ],
    "CacheStatisticsAutoConfiguration.
    EhCacheCacheStatisticsProviderConfiguration": [
  {
    "condition": "OnClassCondition",
    "message": "@ConditionalOnClass did not find required classes
    'net.sf.ehcache.Ehcache',
    'net.sf.ehcache.statistics.StatisticsGateway'"
  }
  ],
```

All these details are very useful in order to debug auto-configuration.

Debugging

Three of the actuator endpoints are useful when debugging problems:

- `/application/heapdump`: Provides a heap dump
- `/application/trace`: Provides a trace of the last few requests serviced by the application
- `/application/dump`: Provides a thread dump

Deploying an Application to Cloud

Spring Boot has great support for most popular Cloud **Platform as a Service (PaaS)** providers.

Some of the popular ones are as follows:

- Cloud Foundry
- Heroku
- OpenShift
- **Amazon Web Services (AWS)**

In this section, we will focus on deploying our application to Cloud Foundry.

Cloud Foundry

The Cloud Foundry Java buildpack has excellent support for Spring Boot. We can deploy standalone applications based on JARs as well as the traditional Java EE WAR applications.

Cloud Foundry provides a Maven plugin to deploy applications:

```
<build>
    <plugins>
        <plugin>
            <groupId>org.cloudfoundry</groupId>
            <artifactId>cf-maven-plugin</artifactId>
            <version>1.1.2</version>
        </plugin>
    </plugins>
</build>
```

Before we can deploy our application, we need to configure the application with a target and a space to deploy the application to.

The following are the steps involved:

- We need to create a pivotal Cloud Foundry account at: `https://account.run.pivotal.io/sign-up`.

- Once we have an account, we can log in at `https://run.pivotal.io` to create an organization and space. Have the org and space details ready as we need them in order to deploy the application.

We can update the plugin with the configuration of `org` and `space`:

```
<build>
    <plugins>
        <plugin>
            <groupId>org.cloudfoundry</groupId>
            <artifactId>cf-maven-plugin</artifactId>
            <version>1.1.2</version>
            <configuration>
                <target>http://api.run.pivotal.io</target>
                <org>in28minutes</org>
                <space>development</space>
                <memory>512</memory>
                <env>
                    <ENV-VAR-NAME>prod</ENV-VAR-NAME>
                </env>
            </configuration>
        </plugin>
    </plugins>
</build>
```

We need to log in to Cloud Foundry using the Maven plugin on command prompt or terminal:

```
mvn cf:login -Dcf.username=<<YOUR-USER-ID>> -Dcf.password=<<YOUR-PASSWORD>>
```

If everything is successful, you will see a message, as shown here:

```
[INFO] ------------------------------------------------------------------
--
[INFO] Building Your First Spring Boot Example 0.0.1-SNAPSHOT
[INFO] ------------------------------------------------------------------
[INFO]
```

```
[INFO] --- cf-maven-plugin:1.1.2:login (default-cli) @ springboot-for-
beginners-example ---

[INFO] Authentication successful

[INFO] ------------------------------------------------------------

[INFO] BUILD SUCCESS

[INFO] ------------------------------------------------------------

[INFO] Total time: 14.897 s

[INFO] Finished at: 2017-02-05T16:49:52+05:30

[INFO] Final Memory: 22M/101M

[INFO] ------------------------------------------------------------
```

Once you are able to log in, you can push the application to Cloud Foundry:

```
mvn cf:push
```

Once we execute the command, Maven will compile, run tests, build the application JAR or WAR, and then deploy it to the Cloud:

```
[INFO] Building jar: /in28Minutes/Workspaces/SpringTutorial/springboot-
for-beginners-example-rest-service/target/springboot-for-beginners-
example-0.0.1-SNAPSHOT.jar

[INFO]

[INFO] --- spring-boot-maven-plugin:1.4.0.RELEASE:repackage (default) @
springboot-for-beginners-example ---

[INFO]

[INFO] <<< cf-maven-plugin:1.1.2:push (default-cli) < package @
springboot-for-beginners-example <<<

[INFO]

[INFO] --- cf-maven-plugin:1.1.2:push (default-cli) @ springboot-for-
beginners-example ---

[INFO] Creating application 'springboot-for-beginners-example'

[INFO] Uploading '/in28Minutes/Workspaces/SpringTutorial/springboot-for-
beginners-example-rest-service/target/springboot-for-beginners-example-
0.0.1-SNAPSHOT.jar'

[INFO] Starting application

[INFO] Checking status of application 'springboot-for-beginners-example'

[INFO] 1 of 1 instances running (1 running)

[INFO] Application 'springboot-for-beginners-example' is available at
'http://springboot-for-beginners-example.cfapps.io'

[INFO] ------------------------------------------------------------
[INFO] BUILD SUCCESS
```

```
[INFO] ------------------------------------------------------------------
[INFO] Total time: 02:21 min
 [INFO] Finished at: 2017-02-05T16:54:55+05:30
 [INFO] Final Memory: 29M/102M
 [INFO] ------------------------------------------------------------------
```

Once the application is up and running on the Cloud, we can use the URL from the log to launch the application: `http://springboot-for-beginners-example.cfapps.io`.

 You can find more information about the Java Build Pack of Cloud Foundry at `https://docs.run.pivotal.io/buildpacks/java/build-tool-int.html#maven`.

Summary

Spring Boot makes developing Spring-based applications easy. It enables us to create production-ready applications very quickly.

In this lesson, we understood the different external configuration options provided by Spring Boot. We looked at embedded servers and deployed a test application to a PaaS Cloud platform--Cloud Foundry. We explored how to monitor our application in the production using Spring Boot Actuator. At the end, we looked at the features that make a developer more productive--Spring Boot developer tools and live reload.

With this, we've come to the end of this book. I hope you'd a smooth journey and gained a lot of knowledge on building microservices with Spring Boot.

I wish you all the best for your future projects. Keep learning and exploring!

Assessments

1. The _____ endpoint provides information about the operating system, JVM installation, classpath, system environment variable, and the values configured in various application properties files.

2. Which of the following is provided by cloud to Cloud Foundry?

    1. Software as a Service

    2. Platform as a Service

    3. Infrastructure as a Service

    4. All of the above

3. State whether True or False: Spring MVC can be extensively configured through `application.properties`.

4. Which of the following actuator endpoints provides a trace of the last few requests serviced by the application when debugging.

   1. `/applications/trace`

   2. `/application/tracing`

   3. `/app/trace`

   4. `/apps/tracing`

5. _____ makes developing Spring-based applications easy as it enables you to create production-ready applications very quickly.

Assessment Answers

Lesson 1: Building Microservices with Spring Boot

Question Number	Answer
1	`SpringApplication`
2	4
3	True
4	1
5	False

Lesson 2: Extending Microservices

Question Number	Answer
1	Bean Validation API
2	4
3	False
4	1
5	3

Lesson 3: Advanced Spring Boot Features

Question Number	Answer
1	environment (env)
2	2
3	True
4	1
5	Spring Boot

www.ingramcontent.com/pod-product-compliance
Lightning Source LLC
Chambersburg PA
CBHW080536060326
40690CB00022B/5149